MARRIAGES

OF

HENRICO COUNTY

VIRGINIA

1680 — 1808

I0091022

Compiled by:

Joyce H. Lindsay

Southern Historical Press, Inc.
Greenville, South Carolina

Please Direct all Correspondence & Orders to:

Southern Historical Press, Inc.
P.O. Box 1267
Greenville, S.C. 29602-1267

FOREWORD

Like James City, Henrico County was named after a town within its limits. In 1611 Sir Thomas Dale, with the permission of acting Governor Thomas Gates, made a settlement of 350 chosen men upon a neck of land on James River. The place, which was nearly surrounded by water, he called Henricopolis or Henrico, in honor of Prince Henry, son of King James. The county formed twenty-three years later received the name of the town, and thus indirectly Prince Henry's name. (Long's Virginia County Names, pp. 31-32.)

Henrico was one of eight original shires and extended "from Charles City County indefinitely westward". This vast territory was not partitioned for nearly one hundred years. In 1727 Goochland, to the west, was formed from Henrico and Buckingham, Cumberland, Fluvanna, Nelson, Powhatan, and parts of Appomattox. In 1749 Chesterfield, on the south side of the James River, was cut off. With one exception, this left the geographical limits of Henrico County as they are known today. In 1918 all of Farrar's Island, with the exception of the site of Henricopolis, was given to Chesterfield County. During the War Between the States this island had been formed by cutting a canal through the neck of land.

The first Order Book of Henrico is not extant and records of the first county officers are not available. The first burgesses to represent Henrico were Captain Thomas Harris, Christopher Branch, and Edward Tunstall in the session that assembled 6 January 1639. (Stanard's Colonial Virginia Register, p. 60.)

In 1680 Varina, on the north side of James River, became the site of the Henrico Courthouse. The court convened there until 1752, at which time it was moved to its present site at twenty-second and Main Streets in Richmond. The Courthouse was burned during the evacuation of Richmond on April 3, 1865, and was rebuilt soon after the war.

The marriage bonds, which begin with 1781, have been beautifully restored and mounted in nineteen large volumes which are individually indexed. In 1916 a master index of the bonds was prepared and this work has been found to be extremely accurate. The page references of this book are to the master index. The very early marriage license returns were searched out of the Deed, Will, and Order Books. The marriages by inference were found in the records of the Orphan's Court.

I wish to extend to Catherine Lindsay Knorr, who has published fourteen volumes of Virginia marriages, my sincere appreciation for her advice and help. I also wish to thank Miss Helen D. Clevenger, Clerk of the Circuit Court, for her courtesy and help, and for allowing me to examine the marriage records of Henrico County.

Joyce H. Lindsay

Mrs. James R. Lindsay
Richmond, Virginia

To

Grace Fuller Knowles

The good friend who shares
so many of my interests.

16 January 1789. Henry ACCOTT and Polley Chandler. Isaac Ramsbottom, guardian of Polly, consents for her and is surety. Wit. Robert Boyd and Leigh Claiborne. p. 1.

9 February 1791. John ACRE and Nancy Maggee, dau. of John Maggee who consents. Sur. Isham Allen. Wit. Jeremiah Timson and John Cappi. Nancy also writes her own consent. p. 1.

17 June 1786. Malory ADAMS and Clary Ayscough. Thomas Potter, guardian of Clary, consents for her and is surety. Wit. Sam'l _____ and Dave East. p. 1.

6 May 1784. Mellery ADAMS and Betsey Bowers, dau. of Christopher Bowers who consents. Sur. James Drummond. p. 1.

5 May 1797. Samuel G. ADAMS and Catherine Innes. Sur. Wilson Allen. p. 1.

13 July 1700. John ADKINS and Ann Childers. Deeds, Wills, etc. 1697-1704. p. 220.

13 August 1807. Absalom AILSTOCK and Sally Ailstock. Sur. Joseph Ailstock. p. 1.

14 January 1806. James D. ALBERT and Abiah Armistead, dau. of Thomas Armistead who is surety. Note: see de BOURBON. p. 25.

2 March 1791. Benjamin ALLEN, Sr. and Martha Jordan, who consents. Sur. Daniel Burton. Benjamin of Cumberland County. p. 2.

22 January 1796. Christian ALLEN and Frances Harwood, who consents. Sur. John Allen. Wit. Peter Bailey. p. 1.

2 March 1790. Flemong ALLEN and Patsey Allen, who consents. Sur. Richard Allen. Wit. John Allen. p. 1.

17 March 1792. Isham ALLEN and Betsey Mosby. Sur. William Mosby. p. 1.

30 January 1792. James ALLEN and Patsey Mosby, dau. of John Mosby who consents. Sur. and Wit. Isham Allen. p. 2.

18 September 1807. James ALLEN and Frances Whitis, dau. of Samuel Whitis who consents. Sur. Obediah Griffin. Wit. George Mathus, Isham Allen, Jesse Gennins. p. 1.

29 May 1793. Jedediah ALLEN and Elizabeth Franklin, dau. of Lucy Franklin who consents. Sur. William Bellamy. Wit. William and Susanna Kendrick. p. 2.

9 February 1793. John ALLEN and Jane Bottomly. Sur. William Parrott. p. 2.

25 January 1806. John ALLEN and Nancy Graves. Sur. John McBride. Wit. George Chesman. p. 1.

16 October 1807. Jones ALLEN and Elizabeth Mettart. Sur. Charles Winegardner. p. 2.

13 December 1794. Littleberry ALLEN and Jane Austin, who writes her own consent. Sur. Reuben Austin. Wit. Richard Allen and Mary Austin. Archibald Austin, brother of Jane, makes affidavit as to her age. p. 2.

7 September 1807. Richard ALLEN and Maria Austin (a free girl of color) Sur. Liston Temple. p. 2.

13 May 1788. Robert ALLEN and Patsy Spear, widow, who writes her own consent. Sur. Richard Allen. Wit. Julius Allen. p. 2.

9 October 1790. William ALLEN and Jane Seaton, dau. of Aug't. Seaton who consents and is surety. p. 1.

29 February 1792. William G. ALLEN and Elizabeth Freeman, dau. of Isham Freeman who consents. Sur. William Allen. p. 1.

11 April 1799. David Allen ALLEY and Nancey Shepperson, dau. of William Shepperson who consents. Sur. John Lacey, Jr. Wit. Samuel P. Johnstone and William Price. p. 2.

25 March 1801. John ALLEY and Effany Boyd. Sur. Anselmn Jones and William Alley. p. 2.

4 January 1790. Reuben ALLEY and Sarah Blalock, dau. of Jeremiah and Eliza Blalock who consent. Sur. Peter Frankling. Wit. Jeremiah Blalock, Jr. Sarah also writes her own consent. p. 2.

15 September 1789. Samuel ALLEY and Elizabeth Newman, dau. of Catherine Newman who consents. Sur. Richard Kimbrough. Wit. Lucy Snead. p. 2.

5 May 1806. Thomas H. ALLEY and Lucy Davenport, his ward. Sur. William Alley. p. 2.

23 March 1793. Samuel ALLINSON and Frances Johnson, who writes her own consent. Sur. John McKim. Wit. Andrew McKim. p. 2.

18 June 1803. Woodford ALVIS and Rebecca Jones, dau. of James Jones who consents. Sur. Robert Morris. Wit. John Sandidge. p. 2.

31 May 1783. John AMBLER and Frances Armistead, dau. of Gill Armistead, deceased. J. Ambler, guardian of John consents for him and is surety. John of Hanover County, son of Edward Ambler, deceased. Wit. John Black and Wilson Miles Cary. p. 2.

19 May 1791. John AMBLER and Lucy Marshall, sister of J. Marshall who consents. Sur. Jaquelin Ambler. John Ambler of James City County. p. 2.

May 1704. Henry ANDERSON and Prudence Stratton. Henry of Prince George County. Deeds, Wills, etc. 1697-1704. p. 450.

15 November 1792. Nathaniel ANDERSON and Mrs. Sarah Rawlings. Sur. George Laughlin. p. 3.

15 July 1698. William ANDERSON and Mary Liggon. Deeds, Wills, etc. 1697-1704. p. 124.

24 December 1793. William ANDERSON and Elizabeth Minor. Sur. George Laughlin. p. 3.

20 December 1785. William ANGEL and Mary Valentine, dau. of James Valentine who consents. Sur. William George. Wit. William Whitlock, John Colins, and Zachariah Valentine. p. 3.

27 March 1806. William ANTHONY (a free black man) and Luvinia Patteson (an Indian). Sur. Thomas C. Richardson. p. 3.

27 December 1800. Lyddall APPERSON and Fanny White, dau. of Nancy White who consents. Sur. William G. Allen. Wit. Henry Cary. p. 3.

23 September 1803. Thomas APPERSON and Susanna Francis. Sur. Benjamin Keiningham. p. 3.

January 1695. John ARCHER and Frances Shippy. Sur. Capt. James Royall. Deeds, Wills, etc. 1688-1697. p. 631.

7 November 1799. Frederick ARGYLE and Rebecca Winston. Sur. Francis Irwin. Wit. And. Stevenson. p. 3.

18 November 1796. Adam ARMSTRONG and Mary Scott. Sur. Benjamin Scott. p. 3.

18 September 1806. Richard E. ARMSTRONG and Betsy Austin, widow, who consents. Sur. Thomas Pittman. Wit. Eliza Austin, Mary G. C. Austin, Chapman Timberlake. p. 3.

By 1681. Henry ASCOUGH and Joane Hughson, widow of Robert Hughson. Orphans Court 1677-1739. p. 7.

July 1696. Peter ASHBROOK, Jr. and Mary Forrest. Sur. Moses Wood. Deeds, Wills, etc. 1688-1697. p. 631.

18 January 1786. Gilbert ATKINSON and Eliza Roach, who writes her own consent. Sur. James Leaker. Wit. Caty Leaker. p. 3.

22 December 1798. James ATKINSON and Elizabeth Smith. Thomas Starke, guardian of Elizabeth, consents for her. Sur. Charles Smith. James of New Kent County. p. 3.

6 March 1806. James H. ATKINSON and Rebecca Vaughan. Sur. Henry Vaughan. p. 3.

16 December 1794. Robert ATKINSON and Polly T. Mayo, dau. of William Mayo, Jr. who consents. Sur. Roger Atkinson, Jr. Robert of Dinwiddie County. p. 3.

21 August 1792. Isaiah ATTKISSON and Lucy Ellis, dau. of Joseph Ellis who consents. Sur. Henry Ellis. Wit. Stephen and Charles Ellis. p. 3.

19 November 1791. Chapman AUSTIN and Betsey Austin, dau. of William Austin, Jr. who consents. Sur. John Austin, Jr. Wit. James and Robert Austin. p. 3.

20 April 1792. John AUSTIN and Sarah Hogg, who writes her own consent. Sur. Joshua Hazelwood. Wit. Pleasant Hazelwood. p. 3.

2 November 1787. William AUSTIN and Mary Trueman, dau. of John Trueman, dec'd. and Susan Trueman who gives her consent. Sur. Richard Trueman. Wit. William Trueman. p. 4.

14 July 1802. David AXLEY and Keziah Davenport. Sur. Edmond Weymouth. p. 4.

7 October 1786. Phillip AYLETT and Betsy Henry, dau. of Patrick Henry who consents. Sur. Isaac Younghusband, Jr. Wit. Mary Woody and Anna C. Dandridge. p. 4.

23 February 1787. John BACHELOT and Mary Conand. Sur. James Frances Conand. p. 5.

1 May 1786. Nathaniel BACON and Elizabeth Meux. Sur. William Waddill. Nathaniel of New Kent County. p. 5.

13 May 1794. Goodrich BAILEY and Anne Lawrence, who consents. Sur. Absolom Lawrence. Wit. Thomas Binford and John Hobson. p. 5.

12 February 1798. Parke BAILEY and Elizabeth Simms, widow. Sur. Richard Burns. p. 5.

19 April 1798. Peter BAILEY and Lucy Harwood, who consents. Nathaniel Childers, guardian of Lucy, also consents and is surety. p. 5.

19 December 1792. Richard BAILEY and Elizabeth Pearce, who consents. Sur. James Redford. Wit. Peter Sharp. p. 5.

1 April 1806. Samuel BAILEY and Lucy White, widow of John White. Sur. and Wit. Thomas White. p. 5.

23 May 1785. William BAILEY and Milley Whitlar, who consents. Sur. Reuben George. Wit. William Whitlock, Joseph Bailey, and Mary C. Whitlar. p. 5.

15 June 1803. William BAILEY and Sarah Redford. Sur. Joseph Foster. p. 5.

11 April 1796. Peter BAINE and Nancy Anderson, dau. of Ben Bellis who consents. Sur. Claiborne Anderson. Wit. Nancy Scott. p. 5.

3 February 1791. Adam BAIRD and Nancy Henley, who consents. Sur. Cha. Winegardner. Wit. James Carney and James Shepherd. p. 5.

5 June 1795. Adam BAIRD and Ann White, of lawful age. Sur. and Wit. James Talley. p. 5.

7 April 1787. James BAKER and Lucy Scott, dau. of William Scott who is surety with John Scott. p. 5.

3 September 1683. John BALL and Elianer Barnett. Deeds, Wills, etc. 1677-1692. p. 252.

31 August 1785. Thomas BALL and Susanna Blunt. Sur. Charles Blunt. Wit. William Whitlock. p. 5.

24 October 1789. Thomas BANKS and Milly Gravitt, who consents. Sur. John Hicks. Wit. B. Webb. p. 5.

3 April 1792. Samuel BARBER and Catherine White. Sur. Tarpley White. p. 5.

27 August 1785. Alexander BARKER and Charity Bracket, dau. of Elizabeth Bracket who consents. Sur. James Freeman. p. 5.

11 March 1786. Nathan BARKER and Mary Lucas, dau. of Aaron Lucas who is surety. p. 5.

7 July 1787. William BARKER and Ursley Fussell, who consents. Sur. David Royster. p. 6.

3 February 1806. William BARKER and Hannath Blith. Sur. John Parker. p. 6.

28 June 1803. Benjamin BARLOW and Nancy Jordan. Sur. Noble Jordan. Benjamin of Chesterfield County. p. 6.

7 February 1788. William BARNARD and Eleanor Harden, of lawful age. Sur. and Wit. George Gray. p. 6.

23 June 1788. Anderson BARNES and Mary Fussell, who consents. Sur. Arthur Giles. Wit. Robert Miller. p. 6.

7 December 1807. Allen BARNETT and Lucretia Wood (free people of color). Sur. Elijah Wood. p. 6.

14 November 1807. David BARNETT and Judy Brown. Sur. Jacob Brown who makes oath Judy is over 21; no relationship stated. Wit. Th. C. Howard. p. 6.

5 November 1782. Thomas BARRET and Elizabeth Campbell. Charles Barret, guardian of Elizabeth, consents for her. Sur. Jacob Ego. Wit. William Whitlock. p. 6.

3 September 1806. Robert BASHALL and Mrs. Harriot Orcher. Sur. Hugh White. p. 6.

22 January 1793. Archad BASS and Polley Hughes. Sur. John Miller. p. 6.

13 December 1797. William C. BASSETT and Nancy Davis, widow of Horatio Davis. Nancy writes her own consent. Sur. John Woodward. Wit. Sally Carter. p. 6.

Before 2 April 1688. Thomas BATTE, Jr. and Temperence Brown, orphan of John Brown. Orphans Court 1677-1739. p. 21.

May 1704. William BATTE and Mary Stratton. William of Prince George County. Deeds, Wills, etc. 1697-1794. p. 450.

21 January 1793. Joseph BAXTER and Mary Cox, who consents. Sur. Thomas Elliott. Wit. John Courtney and W. Foushee. p. 6.

4 July 1788. John BEALLS and Caty Williams, sister of Elisha Williams who gives his consent and is surety with William Green. p. 6.

19 July 1799. John BECKETT and Mrs. Sarah Miller, widow. Sur. Benjamin Phillips and William Slaborne. Wit. Andrew Stevenson. p. 6.

11 December 1795. Archibald BEESON and Sarah Barker, of lawful age. Sur. Jasper Beeson. Wit. Drury Allen. p. 6.

27 July 1793. German BELHOSTE and Elizabeth Sharp, dau. of Robert Sharp who consents and is surety. Wit. James Wray. p. 6.

17 December 1789. George BELL and Sarah Homes, who consents. Sur. Randolph McGee. p. 6.

23 December 1802. William BELL and Mrs. Catherine Maxwell, widow, who consents. Sur. and Wit. Andrew Squair of Albemarle County, brother of Catherine. William of City of Richmond. p. 7.

20 December 1798. John BELLAMY and Patsey Cocke, who writes her own consent. George Pyle and Pleasant Cocke, father of Patsey, certify that she is of age. Sur. George Pyle. Wit. O. Gathright and Nathaniel Thomas. p. 7.

19 April 1806. Elijah BENNETT and Tempe Jones, of the City of Richmond. Sur. Benjamin Jones. p. 7.

22 November 1792. Levy BENNETT and Frances Hughes. Sur. Emery Hughes. Wit. Nathaniel Sheppard. p. 7.

8 October 1787. Nathaniel BENNETT and Rachel Nailor. Sur. James Bennett. Wit. Benjamin Pollard. p. 7.

7 May 1792. Richard BENNETT and Martha Rice, who consents. Sur. William Thorp. Wit. James Bennett and William Royster. p. 7.

4 March 1803. William BENNETT and Mrs. Sally Herbert. Sur. David Johnson. p. 7.

9 November 1790. Nelson BERKELEY and Mary Barret, dau. of John Barret who consents. Sur. and Wit. William Barret. p. 7.

18 April 1792. Charles BERNETT and Mary Juills. Alexander Lory consents for Mary; no relationship stated. Sur. William Parrot. Wit. David Burgess. Note: Bond written Bernett signature is Burnett. p. 7.

20 April 1808. Benjamin BERRY and Elizabeth Taylor, ward of Charles F. Gretter who is surety. p. 7.

8 April 1801. Elisha BETHEL and Rachael Hundley. Sur. James Parkinson. p. 7.

26 December 1788. William BETHEL, Jr. and Rebecca Houal, of lawful age. Sur. Isham Bethel. Wit. Mathew Hobson and Samuel Goode. p. 7.

22 February 1785. Isham BETHELL and Agness Bethell, dau. of William Bethell who consents and states Agness is of lawful age. Sur. John Garthright. p. 7.

30 January 1801. Robert BETHELL and Sarah Wade, dau. of Banks Wade who is surety. p. 7.

20 January 1801. Thomas BETHELL and Agness Bethell, dau. of Jane Bethell who certifies Agness is 26 years of age. Sur. and Wit. William Coghill. p. 7.

31 May 1796. James BINFORD and Elizabeth G. Carter, dau. of Jacob Carter who consents. Sur. Thomas Binford. Wit. John Carter, Jr. p. 7.

15 July 1806. James BINFORD and Elizabeth Garthright, dau. of Ephraim Garthright. Sur. Moses Woodfin. p. 7.

7 March 1800. Sherwood BINFORD and Martha Parker, his ward. Sur. Jonathan Brackett. p. 8.

12 August 1790. Thomas BINFORD and Betsey Bracket, who consents. Sur. James Warinner. Wit. T. S. Claiborne, John Dollard, and Ann Dollard. p. 7.

30 December 1794. Thomas BINFORD and Priscilla Warinner, dau. of John Warinner who consents. Sur. William Pembertone. Wit. John and Sarah Whitlock. p. 8.

14 May 1806. Thomas BINFORD, Jr. and Catharine Price. Sur. William Gathright. p. 7.

6 December 1798. William BINFORD and Sarah Binford, of lawful age. Sur. Moses Woodfin. Wit. Frances Binford, James Binford, and Benjamin Parker. p. 8.

14 October 1807. James BINGHAM and Elizabeth Ellis, widow, who consents. Sur. Jacob G. Ege. Wit. Richard Edwards and B---- Tinner? p. 8.

29 November 1799. James BINNS and Mrs. Ann Thompson, who consents. Sur. John Wells. Wit. Michael S. Bradley. James Binns of Charles City County. p. 8.

17 June 1796. Absolem BLACKBURN and Judy Sneed, of lawful age. Sur. and Wit. Charles Sneed. p. 8.

13 April 1792. John BLACKBURN and Sally Cawthon, who consents. Sur. and Wit. Elisha Jones. p. 8.

25 August 1808. John BLACKBURN and Elizabeth Blalack. Sur. Reuben Alley who makes oath Elizabeth is over 21. p. 8.

6 April 1798. Samuel BLACKBURN and Milly Lucas, dau. of John Lucas who is surety. p. 8.

10 December 1808. Thomas BLACKBURN and Ann Carter Holloway, dau. of John Holloway who is surety. p. 8.

6 September 1785. James BLACKLEY and Mary Jefferson. Sur. John Godfrey. p. 8.

7 October 1785. William BLADES and Betty Baley, who consents. Sur. David East. Wit. Sam Scherer. p. 8.

27 November 1790. James BLAKELEY and Elizabeth Harwood, who consents. Sur. John Amminett. Wit. Sally Hughes Bailey, Nancy Taylor, William Stokeley, Charles Burnett. p. 8.

28 October 1785. John BLAKEY and Jemima Johnson, dau. of Thomas Johnson, Sr. who consents and is surety. p. 8.

February 1701. Richard BLANDE and Elizabeth Randolph. Deeds, Wills, etc. 1697-1704. p. 279.

5 January 1786. Thomas BLOCK and Mary Addison, who consents. Sur. William Bullington. p. 8.

31 May 1790. William BLOCK and Luky Hudson, dau. of Turner H. Hudson who consents. Sur. John Lester. Wit. Joseph Brown. p. 8.

27 June 1806. James BOATWRIGHT and Precilla Murphey, dau. of John Murphey, of the City of Richmond, who is surety. p. 9.

16 February 1785. Joseph BOHORN and Barbara Capeheart, dau. of Peter Capeheart who consents. Sur. James Weaver. p. 9.

29 December 1697. John BOLLING and Mary Kennon. Deeds, Wills, etc. 1697-1699. p. 96.

23 F bruary 1798. William BOLLING and Mary Randolph, of lawful age. Daughter of Richard Randolph, deceased. Sur. Thomas Bolling, father of William. p. 9.

27 May 1785. William BOOKER and Sarah Smith. Sur. Jesse Smith. p. 9.

1 January 1803. Thomas BOOTH and Mrs. Christian James, widow, who consents. Sur. and Wit. William Derrough. p. 9.

14 December 1797. Hazlewood BOTTOM and Ruth Stiff. Sur. William Francis. p. 9.

14 May 1788. Joel BOTTOM and Elizabeth Echo. Isaac and Lucy Echo give their consent; no relationship stated. Sur. and Wit. Pleasant Bottom. p. 9.

14 July 1790. Rowland BOTTOM and Elizabeth Williams, dau. of Rachel Williams who consents. Sur. James Meredith. Wit. Thomas Binford. p. 9.

4 April 1793. John BOURCHETT and Milly Deane, who consents. Sur. James Wray. Wit. Salley Dean. p. 9.

27 July 1793. Peter BOURIENE and Mary Sharpe, dau. of Robert Sharp who consents and is surety. Wit. James Wray. p. 9.

31 January 1788. Jeffrey BOWLES and Sally Morris, dau. of William Morris, deceased. Sur. Robert Morris. p. 9.

21 September 1803. Thomas BOWLES and Rebecca Williamson. Sur. John Williamson. Thomas of Hanover County. p. 9.

24 May 1802. William BOWLES and Verlinche Branch. Sur. John B. Winn. p. 9.

29 June 1790. Charles BOWMAN and Nancy Auldin, wid., who consents. Sur. Francis Bowman. Wit. M. Rawlings and Edward Bowman. p. 10.

28 December 1786. Edward BOWMAN and Catherine Scott, dau. of Robert and Mary Scott who consent. Sur. John Scott and Andrew Scott. p. 9.

15 December 1795. John BOWS and Sarah Allen, dau. of Elizabeth Allen who consents. Sur. Richard Allen. Wit. William and Littleberry Allen. p. 10.

15 December 1800. Gideon BOWSHEN and Patsey Homes, dau. of William Homes who is surety and makes oath Gideon is over 21. p. 10.

17 January 1807. Daniel BOZE and Levinia Melton, dau. of John Melton who certifies Levinia is over 21. Sur. Thomas White. Wit. Henry Warren. p. 10.

27 June 1806. George BRACK and Elizabeth Roane, of the City of Richmond. Sur. John Raines. p. 10.

10 November 1800. Jonathan BRACKETT and Elizabeth Carter. Sur. William Carter, Jr. William Carter makes oath Elizabeth is over 21. p. 10.

13 February 1789. Archelaus BRADLEY and Susanna Lyon Samuel Apperson, guardian of Susanna, consents for her. Sur. Littleberry Royster. Wit. Daniel Lyon. p. 10.

10 June 1808. Francis BRADLEY and Winnefred Liggan, dau. of William Liggan who is surety. p. 10.

24 September 1792. James BRADLEY and Agnes Garthright, who consents. Sur. Joseph Garthright. Wit. Samuel Goode. p. 10.

27 June 1807. James BRADLEY and Sarah Glenn, dau. of William Glenn who is surety. p. 10.

10 March 1803. Littleton BRADLEY and Fanny Baker. Sur. Richard Ragland who makes oath Fanny is over 21. p. 10.

Before 5 October 1725. William BRADLEY and Hester Bridgwater, widow of Thomas Bridgwater. Orphans Court 1677-1739. p. 34.

21 December 1807. William J. BRADLEY and Catherine C. Walker. Sur. Nelson Butler. p. 10.

By 1 October 1695. Christopher BRANCH and Ann Sherman, dau. of Henry Sherman. Deeds, Wills, etc. 1688-1697. p. 595.

Before August 1689. Thomas BRANCH and Elizabeth Archer, orphan of George Archer. Orphans Court 1677-1739. p. 24.

13 April 1793. Robert BRANSFORD and Rachel Courtney, dau. of John Courtney who consents and is surety. Wit. Jane and Elizabeth Courtney. p. 10.

1 January 1791. James BRECKENRIDGE and Ann Selden. Sur. James McClurg. p. 10.

5 March 1799. James BREEDLOVE and Nancy Davis, dau. of Abraham Davis who is surety. p. 10.

30 December 1789. William BREEDLOVE and Ann Williams, who consents. Sur. Andrew Robertson. Wit. John Robinson and George Todd. p. 10.

7 April 1788. Bartlett BREEDON and Nancy Henrotta. Sur. Edward Henrotta. p. 10.

22 August 1782. Patrick BRENEY and Anne Gardner. Robert Gardner consents for Anne; no relationship stated. Sur. Simon Swail. p. 10.

26 March 1785. William BRENT and Elizabeth Jaquelin, dau. of J. Ambler who consents. Sur. John Marshall. p. 10.

26 May 1790. Benjamin BRIAN and Mary Cauthern, who consents. Sur. Richard Powers. Wit. E. Powers, John Courtney. p. 10.

4 February 1782. Charles BRIDGWATER and Lucy Williamson. Sur. Thomas Williamson. p. 10.

25 February 1786. Daniel BRIDGWATER and Grace McAlister, who consents. Sur. John McAlister. Wit. Robert Gibins. p. 10.

15 March 1782. James BRIDGWATER and Elizabeth Stanhope. Sur. John Sheppard. p. 11.

3 February 1792. William BRIDGWATER and Mary Ann Clarke. John Clarke Brook consents for Mary Ann; no relationship stated. Sur. and Wit. Benjamin Clarke. p. 11.

7 October 1785. Reynolds BRIGHTWELL and Sally Evans, of lawful age. Sur. William Evans, brother of Sally. Wit. W. Whitlock, James Craig. p. 11.

30 March 1793. William BRITAIN and Rebecca Cornet. Sur. John Cornet. p. 11.

12

6 December 1798. Charles BRITTAIN and Patsey Brumfield. Sur. George Mann. p. 11.

7 June 1802. Jesse BRITTAIN and Sally Franklin. Sur. Andrew Williams. p. 11.

1 January 1795. John BRITTAIN and Mary Baker. Sur. Martin Baker. p. 11.

26 December 1788. Thomas BROADWAY and Elizabeth Warinner, dau. of Benjamin Warinner who consents. Sur. Samuel Warinner. Wit. John and Joseph Warinner. p. 11.

17 April 1797. John BROCKENBOROUGH and Mrs. Gaberilla Randolph. Sur. Spencer Roane. p. 11.

13 August 1797. Joshua BROTHERHOOD and Dorothy Negley, dau. of Jacob Negley who is surety. p. 11.

9 January 1793. Henry BROUGHTON and Mary Bromwell. Sur. William Bromwell. p. 11.

8 September 1801. Basil BROWN and Elizabeth P. Price. Sur. John Williamson. Basil of King William County. p. 11.

8 October 1792. James BROWN and Mary Taylor, who consents. Sur. Jesse Sadler. Wit. Peter Byzer. Note: Bond reads Mary consent signed Nancy. p. 11.

12 October 1703. John BROWN and Martha Stratton. Deeds, Wills, etc. 1697-1704. p. 351.

17 September 1788. John BROWN and Mary Jude, who consents. Sur. Frederick Jude. Wit. George and Sally Jude. p. 12.

30 October 1795. John BROWN and Mrs. Judith Collins. Sur. Charles Meeks. p. 11.

18 August 1803. John BROWN and Frances Wilson. Sur. Thomas Glenn. p. 11.

18 April 1806. John BROWN, Jr. and Mrs. Charlotte Southall, widow of Charles Southall. Sur. John Brown, Sr. who makes oath Charlotte is a resident of the City of Richmond. p. 11.

25 September 1806. John H. BROWN and Mary Copland, both of the City of Richmond. Sur. John Brown. Wit. E. Copland and P. Copland. Charles Copland, father of Mary, consents for her. p. 11.

31 August 1786. Richard BROWN and Duerzeler Austin, dau. of Thomas Childrey who certifies she is of age. Sur. Thomas Childers and Simon Murray. Wit. Thomas Ripley. p. 12.

22 July 1807. Samuel BROWN and Judith Cottrell, dau. of Charles Cottrell, Sr. who is surety. p. 12.

10 August 1795. William BROWN and Maria Pleasants, wid. Sur. John Pierce, Jr. Wit. Wilson Allan. p. 12.

24 November 1802. William BROWN and Mary Smoot, dau. of Benjamin Smoot who consents. Macajah Brown, father of William, consents for him. Sur. William Castlin. Wit. Robert Priddy and Josiah Smoot. p. 12.

26 October 1807. William BROWN and Catherine Davis, dau. of John Davis who is surety. p. 12.

18 October 1782. Archibald BROWNING and Mrs. Phobe Franklin. Sur. Jacob Thomas. p. 12.

22 April 1803. Robert BROWNING and Mrs. Mary Williamson, who consents. Sur. David Edwards. p. 12.

16 September 1782. Samuel BROWNING and Anne Eubank. Sur. William Browning. p. 12.

21 July 1787. John BRYAN and Agness Cocke, of lawful age. Sur. and Wit. William Cocke. p. 12.

8 January 1794. Wilson BRYAN and Betsey Pearson, dau. of Sarah Pearson who consents. Sur. William Starr. Wit. Henry Starr. p. 12.

31 December 1791. Cornelius BUCK and Judith Hughes, who consents. Sur. John Cunliffe. Wit. Sally Seabrook. p. 12.

9 July 1790. Aylett BUCKNER and Martha Hodges. William King, guardian of Martha, consents for her. Sur. Lewis Buckner, who certifies Aylett is above 21 years of age. Wit. Eli Crim, William Price, John Price. p. 12.

23 January 1801. Josiah BULLINGTON and Maria Hobson, dau. of Matthew Hobson, Sr. who consents. Sur. John Turpin. Wit. Thomas Clopton. p. 12.

28 December 1789. John BURCH and Dorothy Pleasants, dau. of Elizabeth Pleasants who consents. Sur. John Russell. Wit. James Russell. p. 12.

31 December 1794. Thomas BURGESS and Mary Heisler. Sur. William Cook. p. 13.

25 October 1808. Thomas BURGESS and Mary Hughes, widow, who consents. Sur. and Wit. Robert Tyler. p. 12.

23 February 1792. Charles BURNETT and Judith Hill, who consents. Sur. William Parrott. Wit. Thomas Watson, Robert Broaddus. Ann Porter certifies Judith is above the age of 21. p. 13.

6 December 1786. John BURNS and Mary Williams, who consents. Sur. Samuel Archibald. Wit. William Whitlock, Michael McKierney, Shardlow Wightman. p. 13.

2 January 1799. Isaac BURRUSS and Patsey Anne Robinson. Sur. Benjamin Neal and Elijah Franklin. p. 13.

6 June 1798. Cunningham BURTON and Polly Holbert. Sur. William Davidson. p. 13.

15 December 1781. Daniel BURTON and Mary Puryear. Sur. Samuel Pine. p. 13.

24 July 1795. Daniel BURTON and Sally Owen, who consents. Sur. William Burton. Wit. Wilson Allen and Isaac Winston. p. 13.

5 February 1795. Jeremiah BURTON and Arener Nicolson, of lawful age. Sur. Archibald Toney and Samuel Allen. Wit. Charles Pine and Judy Collins. p. 13.

23 March 1785. John BURTON and Frances Anne Pinchback, dau. of Francian Boswell who consents and certifies Frances is of age. Sur. Thomas Pinchback. p. 13.

2 May 1794. John BURTON and Elizabeth Oslin, who consents. Sur. Abraham Dugard. Wit. Sarah --------. p. 13.

10 June 1802. John BURTON and Lucy Frayser, dau. of Jackson Frayser who is surety. p. 13.

8 June 1793. Robert BURTON and Mary Martin, who consents. Sur. John Madison. Wit. John Brown. p. 13.

17 September 1793. Thomas BURTON and Clementina Pleasants, dau. of Elizabeth Pleasants who consents. Sur. Gervais Storrs. p. 13.

Between 1688-1689. William BURTON and Mary Parker. Deeds, Wills, etc. 1688-1697. p. 97.

29 May 1789. Lewis BURWELL and Judith Cannon. John McKeand, guardian of Judith, consents for her and is surety. Wit. Elizabeth McKeand. Lewis of Gloucester County. p. 13.

14 September 1791. Thomas BUTLER and Susanna Carter, who consents. Sur. George Hamblett. Wit. Robert Wilkins and M. Green. p. 13.

7 February 1803. Thomas BUTLER and Nancy Grinstead. Sur. John Ford. p. 13.

12 May 1797. Daniel CALL and Lucy Ambler, dau. of J. Ambler who consents. Sur. William Marshall. Wit. J. Marshall. p. 15.

16 March 1787. William CALL, Jr. and Helen Walker, who consents.
Sur. Brett Randolph. Wit. D. N. Randolph and Ann Walker.
p. 15.

2 April 1791. James CALLIHAM and Mary Sadler, who writes her
own consent. Mary is daughter of Jeremiah Sadler. Sur. Jesse
Sadler. Wit. Richard Burns, Frances Phillips, Patrick Buttler.
p. 15.

31 May 1792. Joseph CAMBY and Sarah Miller, who consents.
Sur. James Roberts. Wit. James Lester and Richard M------.
p. 15.

18 November 1800. Armistead CAMP and Sukey Eubank, dau. of
John Eubank who is surety. p. 15.

17 December 1794. Robert CAMPBELL and Ann Alison, dau. of
Fr's. Alison who consents. Sur. John Hicks. Wit. James
Dickinson. p. 15.

7 September 1808. David T. CANNON and Susan Ball, dau. of
Thomas Ball who consents. Sur. William Carter. Wit. Thomas
Peirs. p. 15.

7 November 1798. Jonas CAPHEART and Polly Oakley. Sur. John
Oakley. p. 15.

17 November 1797. William CARDWELL and Betty Brown, colored,
of lawful age. Kitty Brown, mother. Sur. George Redford.
p. 15.

4 January 1790. James CARNEY and Eughan Thompson, who consents.
Sur. Robert Thompson. Wit. John Clark. p. 15.

19 February 1801. John CARPENTER and Patsey Valentine. Sur.
Joseph May. p. 15.

3 May 1793. Samuel CARPENTER and Naomey Hazlegrove, who consents.
Sur. John White. Wit. Levy Reubin and Ri'd. Mason. p. 15.

8 December 1792. Edward CARRINGTON and Mrs. Elizabeth J. Brent.
Sur. Alexander Buchanan. p. 15.

27 December 1794. William CARSON and Catherine Grantland, who
consents. Sur. Thomas Pinchback. Wit. Michael Grantland.
p. 15.

20 December 1799. Charles CARTER and Elizabeth Blackburn.
Sur. Jesse Blackburn. p. 15.

10 February 1795. John CARTER and Matilda Wray, dau. of James
Wray who consents. Sur. William Hawkins. Wit. Will. Carter,
Sr. p. 16.

22 December 1797. John CARTER and Jane M. Gathright. Sur.
Ellyson Carter. Wit. Mat. Hobson. p. 16.

29 October 1808. Moses CARTER and Elizabeth Royster, dau. of
Littleberry Royster who is surety. p. 16.

17 September 1807. Richard CARTER and Susanna Marion Price,
dau. of John Price who is surety. p. 16.

21 February 1792. Theodorick CARTER and Frances Hobson, who
consents. Sur. Jackson Frayser. Wit. ------- - Purkings.
p. 16.

18 March 1794. William CARTER and Betsey Hobson. Sur.
Matthew Hobson. Wit. Jacob Carter. p. 16.

28 July 1800. William CARTER, Jr. and Elizabeth Harwood,
ward of Tarpley White who consents and is surety. p. 16.

16 December 1799. Henry CARY and Catharine White. Sur.
Samuel Wooddy. p. 16.

22 August 1695. Miles CARY, Jr. and Elizabeth Cocke. Deeds,
Wills, etc. 1688-1697. p. 604.

28 March 1794. Joseph CASKY and Lucy Lewis, who consents.
Sur. Richard Dixon Nailoy. Wit. Charles Lewis, Mary Nailoy.
p. 16.

10 December 1793. Hugh CASSIDY and Fanny Clarke, who consents.
Sur. Joseph Colevill. Wit. Dan'l. Dailey. p. 16.

3 April 1794. Andrew CASTLIN and Mrs. Lucy Lenox, who consents.
Sur. Thomas Murray. Wit. James Turner and Elizabeth Swinton.
p. 16.

25 October 1806. Edward CATLING and Mrs. Elizabeth Day, widow.
Sur. Archelaus Meanley. p. 16.

20 May 1793. John CAUCKWELL and Susanna Thomason. Sur. Samuel
Smith. Wit. William Craig. p. 16.

24 May 1792. William CAWTHON and Sally Bowles, who consents. .
Sur. James Cawthon. p. 16.

22 September 1709. Thomas CHAMBERLAYNE and Elizabeth Stratton,
dau. of Edward Stratton. Deeds & Wills, 1706-1709. p. 188.

27 July 1784. William CHAMBERLAYNE and Margaret Wilkinson.
Sur. Nathaniel Wilkinson. p. 16.

1688. William CHAMBERS and Elizabeth Ferris. Deeds, Wills,
etc., 1688-1697. p. 20.

28 July 1785. William CHANDLER and Sally Mourning, of lawful age. Sur. William Weatherly. Wit. William Whitlock. Edward Warren. p. 16.

6 June 1801. George CHARMAN and Elizabeth Gregory Bennett, dau. of Richard Bennett of the City of Richmond who is surety. p. 17.

3 March 1792. Edmund CHEATHAM and Milly Norment, who consents. Sur. Thomas Kessee. Wit. Peter Sharp and James Redford. p. 17.

21 February 1706. Thomas CHEATHAM and Tabitha Branch, widow. Deeds & Wills, 1706-1709. p. 67.

1 January 1790. John Augustus CHEVALLIE and Sally McGee, of lawful age. Sur. Joseph Latil. Wit. Joseph Gallego. p. 17.

September 1696. Abra. CHILDERS, Jr. and Hester Cannon. Deeds, Wills, etc., 1688-1697. p. 631.

Before 15 September 1708. Henry CHILDERS and Lucretia Jones. Orphans Court, 1677-1739. p. 51.

26 December 1797. James CHILDERS and Mary Matthews. Sur. Thomas Williams. Wit. illegible. p. 17.

23 December 1791. Meredith CHILDERS and Mary Goyne, who consents. Sur. John Goyne. Wit. Aggy Goyne and Richard Loving. p. 17.

1 December 1790. Nathaniel CHILDERS and Sally H. Bailey, who consents. Sur. Pleasant Younghusband. Wit. Frances Harwood, Nancy Taylor, Thomas Harwood, illegible. p. 17.

17 January 1806. Noah CHILDERS and Mary Goode, dau. of John Goode. Sur. Austin Johnson who makes oath both are over 21. p. 17.

12 December 1797. Patrick CHILDERS and Nancy Goyne, dau. of Agnes Goyne. Nancy is of lawful age. Sur. Dudley Minor. Wit. William Richardson. p. 17.

2 June 1792. Robert CHILDERS and Nancy Harwood. Sur. Thomas Harwood. p. 17.

21 October 1786. Abraham CHILDRESS and Sally Foster, of lawful age. Sur. Joseph Parker. Wit. Mary Foster and Warren Redford. p. 17.

1 July 1784. James CHILDRESS and Elizabeth Fussell. Sur. John Fussell. Wit. W. Whitlock. p. 17.

22 July 1800. John CHILDRESS and Anne Austin, who consents. Sur. Richard Allen, who makes oath both are over 21. Wit. Pusey Childress. p. 17.

7 June 1803. John CHILDRESS and Polly Cocke Redford. Sur. Joseph Foster. p. 17.

24 December 1800. William CHILDRESS and Elizabeth Ellis. William Ellis consents for Elizabeth; no relationship stated. Sur. Richard Childress. Wit. Elisha Ellis. p. 17.

19 March 1808. Charles CHILDREY and Eliza Redford, his ward. Sur. John Childrey. p. 17.

1 March 1806. John CHILDREY and Elizabeth H. Frayser, dau. of Jackson Frayser who is surety. William Childrey makes oath John is over 21. p. 17.

6 January 1806. Thomas CHILDREY and Mrs. Ann Pearce, widow of Francis Pearce. Sur. Joseph Bailey. p. 17.

1691. Francis CHOHNELEY (CHOLMLEY) and Sarah Huddlesy. Deeds, Wills, etc., 1688-1697. p. 357.

22 November 1793. Charles CHURCHILL and Dolly French. Sur. Peter Robinson. p. 18.

12 December 1788. John Herbert CLAIBORNE and Mary Gregory, dau. of Roger Gregory. Sur. Richard Gregory. Wit. Roger Gregory, Jr. p. 18.

20 April 1783. William CLAIBORNE and Frances Black. Sur. Arch. Blair. Wit. Adam Craig. p. 18.

21 February 1793. Absalom CLARK and Margaret Durham, who consents. Sur. Nathaniel Clark. Wit. Thomas ----------, Susannah Taylor. p. 18.

8 March 1793. Robert CLARK and Elizabeth Elmore, dau. of Charles Elmore who consents. Sur. William Bellamy. Wit. Thomas Burton. p. 18.

31 October 1807. Archibald CLARKE and Maria Mauzey. Sur. Thomas Clarke who makes oath Maria is over 21. p. 18.

2 March 1796. Benjamin CLARKE and Patty Clark, dau. of Jane Clarke. Patty is of lawful age. Sur. Thomas Lewis, Jr. Wit. Zack Clarke. p. 18.

22 September 1796. Benjamin CLARKE and Franky Freeman, dau. of Richard Freeman who is surety. p. 18.

2 June 1786. George CLARKE and Dolly Bridgewater, who consents. Sur. Daniel Bridgewater. Wit. C. Watkins. p. 18.

27 August 1787. George CLARKE and Mary Bennett. Sur. James Bennett. Wit. Benjamin Pollard. p. 18.

25 January 1785. James CLARKE and Anney Moseley, of lawful age. Sur. Thomas Harris and James Heartless. p. 18.

1 July 1807. John CLARKE and Mary Omberson, widow. Sur. John Craddock. p. 18.

15 August 1789. Josiah CLARKE and Sarah Wright, who consents. Sur. Robert Kettelwele. Wit. William Dickinson and John Parker. p. 18.

17 September 1793. Nathaniel CLARKE and Janie Durham, who consents. Sur. James Brown. Wit. Richard Thompson, John Thompson, Priscilla Hollins. p. 18.

3 March 1785. Obediah CLARKE and Ann Miller, dau. of William Miller who consents and is surety. p. 18.

8 March 1799. Richard CLARKE and Polly Leonard. John Price, guardian of Polly, consents and is surety. p. 18.

18 September 1790. Thomas CLARKE and Martha Goode, who consents. Sur. James Redford. Wit. F. S. Claiborne, Betsey Clarke. p. 18.

16 November 1793. Thomas CLARKE and Sally Taylor Holbert, who consents. Mother of Sally also consents, but signature is illegible. Sur. Royal R. Allen. Wit. Samuel Allen. p. 18.

20 April 1789. William CLARKE and Elizabeth Robinson, who consents. Sur. Thomas Robinson. Wit. John Robertson, Philip Williams. p. 19.

1 June 1791. William CLARKE and Mary Hughes, who consents. Sur. William Williams. Wit. William Johnson, Frances Bennett. James Bennett certifies Mary is over 21. p. 19.

17 July 1795. Zachariah CLARKE and Sally Powell, dau. of William Powell who consents. Sur. William Bridgwater. Wit. Wilson Allen. p. 19.

Before 18 May 1762. John CLARKSON and Susannah Bridgwater, dau. of Joseph Bridgwater. Misc. Records, Vol. 6, p. 1881-1882.

20 January 1693. Allanson CLERKE and Ann Blancheil. Sur. Jas. Cocke. Deeds, Wills, etc., 1688-1697. p. 467.

29 December 1783. David CLOPTON and Mary Ann Vandervall, who consents. Sur. Nicholas Giles. David of New Kent County. p. 19.

22 January 1784. Reuben CLOPTON and Betsy Hales, dau. of John Hales who consents. Sur. George Clopton. Wit. Robert Watkins, John Hales, Jr., Jane Clopton. p. 19.

6 May 1801. Thomas CLOPTON and Lucy Giles, widow of Knowles Giles. Sur. Josiah Bullington. p. 19.

4 January 1808. Bowler F. COCKE and Eliza Agness Pleasants Heth. Sur. Charles L. Wingfield. p. 19.

11 January 1691. James COCKE and Elizabeth Pleasants. Sur. Capt. Thomas Cocke, Jr. and Will Cocke, Jr. Deeds, Wills, etc., 1688-1697. p. 357.

Between 1685-1686. John COCKE and Mary Davis. Deeds, Wills, 1677-1692. p. 389.

24 November 1696. John COCKE and Obedience Branch. Sur. Richard Cocke and Thomas Edwards. Deeds, Wills, etc., 1688-1697. p. 710.

3 July 1782. Richard COCKE and Mrs. Theodocia White. Sur. Samuel Hardy. Richard of Surry County. p. 19.

15 November 1784. Richard COCKE and Sarah Eubank. Sur. James Eubank. p. 19.

18 April 1791. Robert COCKE and Lucy Allen. Sur. Drury Allen. p. 19.

Between 1688-1689. Stephen COCKE and Sarah Marston. Deeds, Wills, etc., 1688-1697. p. 97.

26 May 1694. Stephen COCKE and Martha Banister. Deeds, Wills, etc., 1688-1697. p. 552.

18 March 1793. Thomas W. COCKE and Sally Williamson, dau. of Allen Williamson who consents. Sur. Robert Macartney. Wit. Susanna and Elizabeth Williamson. p. 19.

16 June 1691. William COCKE, Sr. and Sarah Dennis. Deeds, Wills, etc., 1688-1697. p. 253.

2 December 1695. William COCKE and Sarah Perrin. Sur. Thomas Cocke, Sr. Deeds, Wills, etc., 1688-1697. p. 631.

21 August 1795. William COCKRAN and Ann Hooker, who consents. Sur. and Wit. Richard Grinstead. p. 19.

28 September 1789. James COCKROM and Elizabeth Clarke, who consents. Frederick Clark, father of Elizabeth, is surety. Wit. Leigh Claiborne, J. Robinson, Jr. p. 19.

20 April 1695. George COGBILL and El. Blackman. Deeds, Wills, etc., 1688-1697. p. 604.

5 January 1807. Philip COGBILL and Martha Rice, dau. of Richard Rice, deceased. Sur. Richard Cottrell. p. 19.

5 October 1797. William COGHILL and Betsey Bethell, dau. of William Bethell who consents. Sur. Robert Bethell. Wit. John Turner and Moses Hobson. p. 19.

1 December 1789. Jacob COHEN and Peggy Hosher, who consents. Sur. John Howard. Wit. illegible. p. 19.

27 February 1784. John COLE and Rebecca Hogg, who consents. Sur. ------- Thompson. Wit. R. Watkins and William Wilson. p. 19.

25 November 1783. Walker King COLE and Sally Mitchell. William Winston and Mary Curd, guardians of Sally, consent for her. Sur. Robert Mitchell. p. 19.

3 July 1783. Samuel COLEMAN and Susanna Pleasants Storrs. Sur. Archibald Stuart. p. 19.

8 November 1797. Walter COLES and Eliza F. Cocke, dau. of Bowler Cocke who consents and is surety. p. 19.

16 June 1795. Didier COLIN and Catherine Naigley, dau. of Jacob Naigley who consents and is surety. p. 19.

13 February 1790. Edward COLLIER and Elizabeth Hutchinson. Sur. Robert Collier who certifies Eliza is above 21. p. 19.

6 July 1789. James COLLINS and Sarah McMillan, dau. of William Jones who consents and is surety. Wit. John Robinson, Jr. and Samuel White. p. 20.

11 September 1789. John COLLINS and Ann Richardson, who consents. Sur. Charles Boyle. Wit. Simon Murry. p. 20.

14 January 1692. Jacob COLSON and Mary Davis. Deeds, Wills, etc. 1688-1697. p. 435.

15 October 1785. Rawleigh COLSTON and Elizabeth Marshall, sister of John Marshall who consents. Sur. John Beale. p. 20.

26 December 1792. Thomas CONNOR and Jane Jarman, widow, who consents. Sur. David Welsh. Wit. William R. Drinkard. p. 20.

15 November 1806. John L. COOK and Elizabeth O. Darrons, dau. of John Darrons whois surety. p. 20.

2 March 1784. Matthew COOK and Polly Pinchback, dau. of Francisan Bosevell who consents. Sur. John Roper. p. 20.

17 April 1793. Aron COOKE and Fanny Bracker, of lawful age.
Sur. Dedier Collins. Wit. George Bates, Elizabeth --------
p. 20.

23 August 1783. Edward COOKE and Sarah Castel. Sur. Andrew
Castel. p. 20.

6 November 1806. John COOKE and Polly Johnson. Sur. John
Craddock. p. 20.

11 August 1792. David COOPER and Nancy Scott, who consents.
Sur. and Wit. Robin Smith. p. 20.

20 January 1787. James CORDELL and Mrs. Jane Gathright, widow,
who consents. Sur. Turner H. Hudson. Wit. Joseph Bradley.
p. 20.

21 July 1800. Daniel CORKER and Frances Haynes, widow. Sur.
George Dunlevy. p. 20.

23 September 1788. William CORLING and Elizabeth Pate, who
consents. Sur. William Nice. Wit. Matthew Pate. p. 20.

9 August 1797. Allen CORNET and Frances Eubank, dau. of
Joseph Eubank who is surety. p. 20.

12 December 1796. Francis CORNETT, Jr. and Rebecca Browning,
who consents. Sur. William Glenn. Wit. Sally Walton. p. 20.

18 September 1806. William CORNETT and Polley Lewis Britton,
who consents. Sur. William Glenn. p. 20.

25 September 1799. Charles COTTRELL, Jr. and Mary Sheppard,
widow. Sur. John Cook and Samuel Brown. Wit. Andrew
Stevenson. p. 20.

15 September 1806. Charles COTTRELL and Eliza Potts, dau. of
John Potts who is surety. p. 20.

20 January 1808. Peter COTTRELL, Sr. and Rachel Carlisle, dau.
of Samuel Carlisle. Sur. Bernard Reynolds. Rachel Moore makes
oath Rachel was 21 on September last. Wit. John Shelton.
p. 20.

18 September 1795. Richard COTTRELL and Milley Toler, dau. of
Charles Toler who consents. Richard, son of Richard Cottrell
who consents. Sur. Julius Crump. Wit. Susannah Cottrell and
W. Allen. p. 20.

8 January 1800. Richard COTTRELL and Ann Clarke, who consents.
Sur. Peter Cottrell. Wit. Richard Cocke. p. 21.

1 December 1806. William COTTRELL and Sally DuVal. Sur. Peter
Cottrell. p. 21.

13 February 1787. William COULTER and Elizabeth Britton, dau. of Samuel Britton who consents. Sur. Richard Taylor. Wit. Louvick Britton, James Royall, John Royall. p. 21.

27 June 1793. Richard P. COURTNEY and Patsey Brazeal, who consents. Sur. James Bissell. Wit. James Plant, John Turpin, John Tatum. p. 21.

5 May 1788. Nathaniel COUSINS and Kitty Miles, dau. of Henry and Sarah Miles who consent. Sur. John Swepton. Wit. William Liggin. p. 21.

17 September 1799. Reuben COUTTS and Jane New. Sur. John New. Wit. Andrew Stevenson. p. 21.

29 March 1785. Abraham COWLEY and Margaret Tankard. Sur. John Brooke. p. 21.

22 October 1697. George COX and Martha Stratton, dau. of Edward and Martha Stratton. Deeds, etc., 1697-1699. p. 96.

13 June 1791. John COX and Elizabeth Money, dau. of Zack? Money who consents. Sur. Drury Wood. Wit. Elisha Owen and Christopher Stanley. p. 21.

10 April 1789. Redford COX and Mary Bullington, of lawful age. Sarah Bullington, mother of Mary, gives her consent. Sur. Milner Redford. Wit. Francis Bullington. p. 21.

8 December 1787. William COX and Rachel Mathews, widow. Sur. Aaron Smith. Wit. Claiborne Watkins. p. 21.

25 September 1682. John COXE and Mary Kennon. Deeds, Wills, etc., 1677-1692. p. 225.

19 June 1793. John CRADDOCK and Betsey Jackson Depriest. Sur. John Hague. p. 21.

20 December 1792. Robert CRADDOCK and Elvey Roper, who consents. Sur. John Roper. p. 21.

3 January 1793. John CRAWFORD and Catherine Stements, who consents. Sur. Joseph McLaughlin. Wit. Dedier Colin. p. 21.

22 September 1792. James CRAWLEY and Elizabeth Haynes. Sur. Stephen Haynes. p. 21.

4 June 1798. David CRENSHAW and Louisa Brittain, of lawful age. Sur. Lyddall Britton. Wit. William Mays, Jr., John Davis, James Royall. p. 21.

16 December 1806. James CREW and Pamela Earnest, orphan of Samuel Earnest. Waddy Vines, guardian of Pamela, is surety. p. 21.

13 December 1800. Gerrard CRITTENDON and Ann Frances, dau. of Joseph Frances who consents. Sur. John Williams. Wit. John Edwards. p. 21.

27 September 1798. John CRITTENDON and Elizabeth Bottom, widow, who consents. Sur. David Toms. Wit. Thomas Apperson and Frances Barker. p. 22.

1 August 1786. Robert CROLL and Fanny Sanders, who consents. Sur. John Collins. Wit. Robert Crow, William Whitlock, Judy Hobert. p. 22.

23 September 1695. Roger CROSDAIL and Rachell Ruck. Deeds, Wills, etc., 1688-1697. p. 604.

10 February 1800. Nicholas Martin CROTS and Mary Humphries. Sur. John Elliott who makes oath Mary is over 21. p. 22.

16 May 1788. Richard CROUCH and Mary Galt, who consents. Sur. Jacob Ego. Wit. Elizabeth Galt, B. Galt, G. Galt, David Miller, John ----------. p. 22.

25 March 1784. Samuel CROUCHFIELD and Mildred Clarke. Sur. Matthew Hobson, who consents for Mildred; no relationship stated. p. 22.

5 November 1808. Abner CRUMP and Ann Allen. Sur. Christian Allen. p. 22.

3 December 1793. Julius CRUMP and Letitia Lancaster, who consents. Sur. Joseph Simpson. Wit. William Watson and Joseph Lancaster, father of Letitia. p. 22.

23 September 1782. Thomas CRUMPTON and Elizabeth Francis. Sur. Richard Allen. p. 22.

9 July 1798. Turner CRUTCHFIELD and Nancy Wade, who consents. Sur. Thomas Wade. Wit. Richard Allen and Joseph Wade. p. 22.

6 October 1789. John CUNLIFFE and Easter Hughes. Robert Mitchell, guardian of Easter, consents and is surety. p. 22.

3 August 1787. Hugh CURAY and Mary Donnelly, widow. Sur. John Richardson. p. 22.

23 September 1789. Jesse CURD and Jane Ellis, dau. of John Ellis who consents and is surety. Wit. T. S. Claiborne and J. Robinson, Jr. p. 22.

26 June 1782. Bennett CURLE and Isabella Binns, dau. of David Binns, who consents. Sur. and Wit. Sherwood Ligon. p. 22.

12 October 1807. James CURRIE and Caroline R. Pickett, dau. of George Pickett who is surety. p. 22.

6 February 1795. William DABNEY and Mehetible Hylton, dau. of
Daniel L. Hylton who consents. Sur. Nathaniel Sheppard.
p. 25.

11 February 1793. James DAILEY and Betsey Ann Glenn, of lawful
age. Daughter of Craner Glenn who consents. Sur. William
Glenn. Wit. Robert Laughlin and Richardson Glenn. p. 25.

3 April 1785. William DAILEY and Rachel Peters. Sur. Matthew
Richardson. p. 25.

27 September 1794. William DAILEY and Sally Painter, who
consents. Sur. Bob Cooley. Wit. And. Ronald and And.
Leiper. p. 25.

30 October 1806. John DAMES and Mabil Walthal Bailey, dau.
of William Bailey who is surety. p. 25.

22 February 1782. John DANDRIDGE and Elizabeth Booth, dau. of
Tho. Booth who consents. Sur. and Wit. Robert Dandridge.
John of Hanover County. p. 25.

27 May 1802. William DANDRIDGE, Jr. and Sally Webb Cocke, dau.
of Bowler Cocke who consents and is surety. p. 25.

7 March 1785. Lewis Abraham DANLY and Jane Allegre, dau. of
Jane. Sur. Paul Carrington. Wit. Sophia Allegre. p. 25.

24 March 1798. James DANNELS and Susanna Blackburn, who
consents. Sur. and Wit. George Melton. p. 25.

27 February 1808. Richard DARBY and Sally Breeden. Sur.
Bartlett Breeden. p. 25.

17 August 1803. Thomas DARBY and Jane Clarke, dau. of James
Clarke, deceased. Sur. Jackson Darby. Anne Clarke makes oath
her daughter, Jane, is over 21. p. 25.

26 April 1786. John DARRONS and Nancy Prosser, dau. of William
Prosser who consents. Sur. John Strobia. Wit. William
Whitlock, Elizabeth Prosser, Charles Burch. p. 25.

28 December 1791. George DAVENPORT and Susanna Brazeal, who
consents. Sur. George Richardson. Wit. John Jenkins, J.
Robinson, William Gemmell, Charles Hoit. p. 25.

13 September 1802. Caleb M. DAVID and Mary Ann Drewing, who
consents. Sur. Daniel Woodson and O. Gathright. p. 25.

21 January 1788. Brackett DAVIS and Sally Brackett, of lawful
age; dau. of Betsey Brackett. Sur. Thomas Broadway. Wit.
William Binford. p. 25.

29 February 1695. John DAVIS and Elizabeth King. Sur. Capt. Thos. Cocke, Jr. Deeds, Wills, etc., 1688-1697. p. 631.

29 December 1794. John DAVIS and Sarah Brittain, who consents. Sur. and Wit. John Brittain. p. 25.

29 December 1806. John DAVIS and Martha Puckett, widow. Sur. Elisha Toler. p. 25.

13 December 1806. John DEANE and Martha Brack. Sur. John Raines who makes oath Martha is over 21. p. 25.

14 January 1806. Louis Edward Prince DE BOURBON (alias James D. Albert) and Abiah Armistead, dau. of Thomas Armistead, who is surety. p. 25.

3 October 1798. Aubin DE LA FOREST and Betsey Lipscomb. Sur. M. B. Porteaux. Moses Lipscomb, brother of Betsey, makes oath she is over 21. p. 26.

21 November 1789. Robert DEMPSTER and Nancy Anderson, who consents. Sur. William Anderson. Wit. John Martin and William Anderson. p. 26.

7 July 1806. Benjamin DENNIS and Rebecah Martyn, of the City of Richmond. Robert Davidson consents; no relationship stated. Sur. Thomas Pittman. Wit. G. Graham. p. 26.

10 February 1798. Henry DENSEL and Jenny Slate. Sur. Thomas Graham. Wit. William Richardson. p. 26.

25 March 1782. John DEPRIEST and Sarah Turpin, of lawful age. Sur. Richard Crouch. Wit. Abram Redford. p. 26.

21 December 1808. William DEPRIEST and Eliza Lewis, ward of Wiltshire M. Lewis who is surety. p. 26.

26 December 1786. Brazile DEROME and Hannah Patrick. Sur. Francis Graves. Wit. William Whitlock and Rob Boyd. p. 26.

26 April 1785. Lewis DETCHEAUX and Mrs. Mary Perkins. Sur. and Wit. Joseph Downes. p. 26.

10 November 1792. Alexander Gillaume DE VEAUPRE and Agatha de St. Cels, dau. of Marie de St. Cels, who consents. Sur. William Marshall. p. 101.

12 January 1801. Thomas DIDDESS and Clara Pinkney, widow. Sur. George Greenhow. p. 26.

25 March 1790. George DIXON and Jane Pearman, of lawful age; dau. of Jean Pearman. Sur. James Pearman. Wit. Elizabeth Goodman. p. 26.

22 December 1804. George W. DIXON and Elizabeth Berminghan. Sur. John Dixon who makes oath Elizabeth is over 21. p. 26.

25 August 1792. John DIXON and Sarah Valentine. Sur. David Lambert. p. 26.

21 June 1790. Thomas F. DIXON and Alice Clarke, widow, who consents. Sur. Joseph Downs. Wit. Charles Bennett. p. 26.

7 December 1789. John DOLLARD and Ann Baker, who consents. Sur. Anselmn Garthright. Wit. James Binford and James Warinner. p. 26.

30 July 1787. Thomas DONNELLY and Jane Douglas, of lawful age. Sur. Francis Hyland. Wit. Edw. Warren. p. 26.

30 December 1789. Joseph DORTON and Sarah Clarke, dau. of Frederick Clark who consents and is surety. p. 26.

31 May 1787. Reubin DORTON and Martha Allen, both of lawful age. Sur. and Wit. Isham Allen. p. 26.

10 February 1791. Ballaiser DOUSCH and Martha Hubbard. Sur. Thomas Walker. Wit. illegible. p. 26.

19 April 1791. James DOVE and Julilie Omohundro, dau. of Mary Thompson. Sur. John Cunliffe. Wit. Richard Thompson. p. 27.

20 December 1806. Collin DOWDALL and Sarah Barker. Sur. John Lewis who makes oath Sarah is over 21. p. 27.

30 November 1808. Samuel DOYLE and Theodocia Galden. Sur. Theodore Doyle who makes oath Theodocia is over 21. p. 27.

6 May 1806. Henry DRAKE and Elizabeth Philips, ward of Henry. Sur. Thomas Pinchback. p. 27.

5 October 1796. William DRAKE and Amey Morris, of lawful age. Sur. Thomas Pinchback. Wit. W. Allen and William Clanton. p. 27.

13 May 1783. James DRUMMOND and Peggy Boughs. Sur. Christopher Boughs. Wit. William Whitlock. p. 27.

6 December 1788. James DUKE and Mary Muncas, who consents. Sur. Jesse Bowles. Wit. Amy Pettus, To. O. Pettus, ------- Muncas. p. 27.

2 February 1788. Marston DUKE and Nancy Kelly, dau. of Thomas Kelly who consents. Sur. Charles Blunt. Wit. John Kelly. p. 27.

16 December 1806. Richard DUKE and Polly Thompson. John Stagg, guardian of Polly, consents for her. Sur. and Wit. Joseph Taylor. p. 27.

6 December 1800. William DUNAUGH and Betsey Muncas. Sur. Robert Thompson who makes oath Betsey is over 21. p. 27.

9 March 1786. Samuel DUNN and Martha Ratliffe, of lawful age. Sur. and Wit. Francis Ratliffe, brother of Martha. p. 27.

14 October 1784. Andrew DUNSCOMB and Philadelphia Duval. William Duval, guardian of Philadelphia, consents for her. Sur. Zeph. Turner. Wit. Samuel Duval and Caty Pope. p. 27.

4 April 1785. Benjamin DUVAL and Elizabeth Warrick, dau. of Mary Warrick who consents. Sur. James Warrick. Wit. William Duval, William Warrick, A. Dunscomb, Samuel Duval. p. 27.

28 September 1801. Benjamin DUVAL and Patsy Turpin. Sur. Henry Holman. p. 27.

7 April 1801. Joseph DUVAL and Mourning Holman. Sur. Nath. Holman, Jr. Anderson Howerton makes oath Mourning is over 21. p. 27.

5 October 1808. Stephen DUVALL and Lucy Johnson. Sur. Barvel Sharp. p. 27.

Before 20 August 1711. John EASLY and daughter of Jeremiah Benskin. Orphans Court, 1677-1739. p. 53.

28 June 1783. David EAST and Sally Lipscomb. Sur. William Lipscomb. p. 29.

27 September 1786. David EAST and Ann Ayscough, who consents. Sur. and Wit. Thomas Potter. p. 29.

Between 1685-1686. Thomas EAST and Dorothy Thomas. Deeds & Wills, 1677-1692. p. 389.

19 April 1695. Thomas EAST, Jr. and Ann Perrin. Deeds, Wills, etc., 1688-1697. p. 604.

14 June 1799. William ECHO and Susanna Wade, dau. of Benjamin Wade who is surety. p. 29.

13 April 1786. Jacob ECKHARD and Prescilla Bryan, dau. of Obedience Bryan. Prescilla is of lawful age. Sur. Charles Richter. Wit. William Fames. p. 29.

31 April 1699. John EDLOE and Martha Hatcher. John of James City County. Deeds, Wills, etc., 1697-1704. p. 152.

14 February 1789. Edward B. EDWARDS and Mary Scott, dau. of Robert Scott who consents. Sur. John Scott and Edward Bowman. Wit. John Turpin, James Talman, Elizabeth Woodcock. p. 29.

14 May 1785. Francis EDWARDS and Mrs. Sarah Ross, widow, of lawful age. Sur. Simon Murray. Wit. Sarah S. Ross. p. 29.

24 February 1788. John EDWARDS and Adniss Warinner, dau. of John Warinner who consents. Sur. John Williams. Wit. Prescilla Warinner. p. 29.

21 February 1792. John EDWARDS and Betsey Green, who consents. Sur. Benjamin Philips. Wit. Joseph Harkel. p. 29.

30 January 1797. John EDWARDS and Mrs. Ann Robinson. Sur. William Evans. p. 29.

29 April 1785. Lewis EDWARDS and Mary Danforth. Sur. William Waddell. p. 29.

13 June 1808. Lewis S. EDWARDS and Patsy Brittain, widow. Sur. John Lakenan. p. 29.

26 October 1692. Thomas EDWARDS and Martha Osborne. Sur. Edw. Hatcher and Thos. Holmes. Deeds, Wills, etc., 1688-1697. p. 435.

8 March 1784. Jacob EGE and Elizabeth Stubblefield. Edward Stubblefield, guardian of Elizabeth, consents for her. Sur. Pratt Hughes. Wit. Thomas Ballard. p. 29.

26 May 1694. Thomas ELAM and Elizabeth Bevin. Deeds, Wills, etc., 1688-1697. p. 552.

17 December 1798. Cornelius ELLETT and Frances Byons. Sur. Benjamin Sheppard who makes oath Frances is over 21. p. 29.

14 June 1808. John ELLIOTT and Mary Blount. Sur. John Allen who makes oath Mary is over 21. p. 29.

10 December 1792. Charles ELLIS and Nancy Ellis, dau. of Thomas Ellis who consents. Sur. Henry Ellis. Wit. Daniel DuVal and Stephen Ellis. p. 29.

15 December 1798. Daniel ELLIS and Susanna Ellis, dau. of John Ellis. Sur. Henry Ellis. p. 29.

9 April 1798. George ELLIS and Elizabeth Williams, dau. of Elisha Williams who is surety. p. 29.

6 June 1786. James ELLIS and Nancy Blalock, who consents. Sur. Joseph T. Downes. Wit. Marry Blalock. p. 29.

17 November 1801. Samuel ELLIS and Elizabeth Ellis, dau. of Thomas Ellis, deceased. John Patterson, guardian of Elizabeth, consents for her. Sur. Charles Ellis. p. 29.

6 October 1800. Jesse ELLYSON and Susanna Hooper, dau. of John Hooper. Sur. John Boatwright who makes oath Susanna is over 21. p. 30.

20 May 1786. Charles ELMORE and Mary Glenn, dau. of Matthew Glenn who consents. Sur. Cornelius Toler. Wit. William Glenn and Richardson Glenn. p. 30.

12 February 1795. Edward ENROUGHTY and Salley Newman, who consents. Sur. Zebulon Franklin. Wit. John Hooper. p. 30.

7 January 1796. Edward ENROUGHTY and Mary Hibdon, who consents. Sur. Claiborne West. Wit. Nathan Enroughty. p. 30.

24 December 1798. William ENROUGHTY and Polly Redford, who consents. Sur. Anderson Barnes. Wit. Lucy Redford. p. 30.

18 October 1803. George EUBANK and Susanna Holloway. Sur. Allen Cornett. p. 30.

21 October 1803. Hezekiah EUBANK and Betsey Gennett, dau. of Thomas Gennett who consents. Sur. George Dunlevey. Wit. George Chesman and Alex B. Shelton. p. 30.

21 October 1783. James EUBANK and Mary Ann Browning, of lawful age. Sur. and Wit. Samuel Browning. p. 30.

19 June 1794. John EUBANK and Sally Clark, who consents. Sur. Nathaniel Staples. Wit. William Staples, John Staples, James Brown. p. 30.

25 November 1794. Joseph EUBANK and Elizabeth White, dau. of Henry White who is surety. p. 30.

6 March 1798. James EVANS and Sally Trueman, of lawful age. Sur. Fleming Allen. Wit. James Blagrove, Hez. Henley. p. 31.

5 February 1782. Roderick EVANS and Elizabeth Minson, orphan of Henry Minson. Moses Lindsey, guardian of Elizabeth, consents for her and is surety. p. 31.

21 February 1792. Roderick EVANS and Mary Godfrey, who consents. Sur. William Evans. Wit. Sherwood Carter and William Austin. p. 31.

26 January 1785. William EVANS and Lovoisy Minson, of lawful age. Sur. Rhodarick Evans. Wit. William Whitlock and James Craig. p. 31.

27 January 1696. John EVINS, Jr. and Sarah Batt. Sur. Peter Jones and Stephen Cocke. Deeds, Wills, etc., 1688-1697. p. 710.

29 December 1697. John FALES (FAIL) and Mary Elam, widow. Deeds, etc., 1697-1699. p. 96.

16 February 1791. Charles FARIS and Patcey Harlow, dau. of John and Patsy Harlow who consent. Sur. Richard Loving. Wit. John Davis. p. 33.

14 August 1787. William FARIS and Alsey Hughes, who consents.
John and Lucy Faris, parents of William. Sur. John Goine.
p. 33.

31 January 1789. Bowler FARISS and Frances Lyon. Samuel
Apperson, guardian of Frances, consents for her. Sur. Callam
Fariss. Wit. Carter Fariss and William Austin. p. 33.

28 December 1786. Robert C. FARISS and Crania Fariss, dau. of
William Fariss, who consents and is surety. p. 33.

7 July 1788. John Joseph FARRA and Sarah Henley, dau. of
Leonard Henley who consents. Sur. and Wit. Hezekiah Henley.
p. 33.

11 November 1691. John FARRAR and Tempe Batte. Sur. Richard
Jones and Jos. Pattison. Deeds, Wills, etc., 1688-1697. p. 357.

Between 1685-1686. Thomas FARRAR and Katharine Perrin. Deeds
& Wills, 1677-1692. p. 389.

6 September 1792. John FARRIS and Sally Bird, of lawful age.
Sur. John Goine. Wit. David Goine, Sally Bird, Richard
Loving. p. 33.

19 December 1797. Callom FARRISS and Obedience Goode, dau. of
Samuel Goode who consents. Sur. Joseph Garthright. Wit.
William Binford. p. 33.

16 December 1794. Barnaby FIGG and Mrs. Weston Wilkins, who
consents. Sur. Phillip Goff. Wit. John Elliott. p. 33.

10 May 1788. Thomas FINDLEY and Phebe Liggon, dau. of Hannah
Liggon. Samuel Findley, guardian of Phebe, consents for her.
Sur. Nathaniel Cousins. Wit. Hamner Liggon, Jerry Ligon,
William Logen. p. 33.

30 May 1795. George FISHER and Anne Ambler, dau. of J. Ambler
who consents. Sur. Robert Carrington. Wit. Ed. Carrington.
p. 33.

25 May 1807. Luke Francis FISHER and Susanna Myers, wid. Sur.
Colin Dawdle who makes oath Susanna is over 21. p. 33.

23 December 1796. William FISHER and Patsey Trueman, who
consents. Sur. William Fussell. Wit. Wilson Allen, Thomas
Bethell, Nancy Royster. p. 33.

20 January 1791. William H. FITZWHILSON and Mrs. Sarah
Ferguson. Sur. William Ross. p. 33.

12 March 1803. John FLOWERS and Nancy Stewart, widow. Both
of the City of Richmond. Sur. Matthew Connally. p. 33.

31 March 1806. Adam FLOYD and Nancy Berry (both free people of color). Sur. Samuel Cole. p. 33.

20 December 1787. Bartlet FORD and Susanna Blackburn, of lawful age. Sur. and Wit. William Blackburn. p. 34.

28 May 1789. John FORD and Mary Shepperson, of lawful age; dau. of Morning Shepperson. Sur. Francis Shepperson. Wit. F. L. Claiborne, Culberth Ford, William Ford. p. 34.

5 February 1798. John FORD and Agness Holaway. Sur. Francis Shepardson. p. 34.

26 May 1802. Lankston FORD and Elizabeth Jones. Sur. John Burton. Lankston of Hanover County. p. 34.

10 December 1806. Reubin FORD and Nancy E. Smith, dau. of Stephen Smith. Hezekiah Ford, father of Reubin, consents for him. Sur. William Ford. Wit. Jeremiah Burton. p. 34.

13 May 1786. Ryland FORD and Elizabeth Waddill, of lawful age. Sur. John Ford. Wit. C. Watkins, James Waddill, Hannah Waddill. p. 34.

15 June 1801. Ryland FORD and Sally Gennett, dau. of Thomas Gennett who is surety. p. 34.

14 January 1796. William FORD and Elizabeth Woodward. Samuel Woodward consents and is surety. Wit. Wilson Allen. p. 34.

28 March 1789. Samuel FORDE and Agness Blackburn, who consents; dau. of Judah Lucas. Sur. Cuthbert Forde. Wit. William Blackburn, John Ford, William Ford. p. 34.

28 August 1788. Tarlton FORDE and Nancy Thowaton, who consents. Sur. Frederick Jude. Wit. Sally Jude, James Thowaton. p. 34.

2 September 1799. John FOSTER and Judith Redford. Sur. William Pierce. p. 34.

22 December 1790. Joseph FOSTER and Ruth Redford, dau. of William Redford who consents. Sur. Pearin Redford and Leigh Claiborne. p. 34.

8 July 1791. Turner FOSTER and Lucresey Williams, who consents. Sur. Abraham Childress. Wit. Pearin Redford, Abraham Sharp. p. 35.

27 August 1808. Nathaniel FOX and Susan Bockins, widow, who signs her own consent. Nathaniel of King William County. p. 35.

1 June 1790. William FRANCESS and Lucy Brackett, of lawful age; dau. of Elizabeth Brackett. Sur. Jonathan Brackett. Wit. Thomas Binford. p. 35.

5 May 1806. John FRANCIS and Kitty Francis. Sur. William Jarvis who makes oath Kitty is over 21. p. 35.

21 June 1782. Thomas FRANCIS and Susanna Bottom, of lawful age. Sur. and Wit. Richard Allen. p. 35.

27 December 1799. William FRANCIS and Elizabeth Carter, who consents. Sur. Theodorick Carter. Wit. James Blagrove and Ann Carter. p. 35.

9 September 1801. William FRANCIS and Betsey West, widow of John West. Sur. George Walton. p. 35.

25 November 1791. Gilley FRANKLIN and Elizabeth Browning, who consents. Sur. William Thorp who certifies Elizabeth is under 21, is an orphan, and was brought up in his family. p. 35.

16 January 1801. James FRANKLIN and Rebecca Perkins. John Hammil makes oath Rebecca is over 21. Sur. Joshua West. p. 35.

24 December 1785. John FRANKLIN and Nancy Minor. Sur. Zachariah Franklin. Wit. Edward Warren. p. 35.

14 November 1789. Joseph FRANKLIN and Mary Jennings, who consents. Sur. William Acree. Wit. John and Joshua Acree. p. 35.

12 February 1807. Josiah FRANKLIN and Lucy White, who writes her own consent. Sur. Daniel P. Harwood. Wit. Edmund New. p. 35.

23 May 1795. Miles FRANKLIN and Sarah Johnson, dau. of Robert and Mary Johnson who consent. Sur. Robert Johnson. Wit. John Harrel and William Slaborn. p. 35.

29 July 1794. Thomas FRANKLIN and Dolley Ford. Sur. Samuel Ford. p. 35.

17 December 1785. Peter FRANKLING and Barbary Lynch, dau. of Mary Lynch who consents. Sur. Zack. Frankling. p. 35.

4 January 1790. Charles FRANZISINI and Rosetta Brumfield, who consents. Sur. John Bigar. Wit. Dabney Williamson and Nath. Childers. p. 35.

1 March 1806. Benjamin FRAYSER and Nancy Parrish (a free mulatto woman). Benjamin was emancipated by George Frayser of Hanover County. Sur. Isham Winn. p. 36.

13 November 1783. Jesse FRAZIER and Kesiah Hobson. Sur. William Frazier. p. 36.

23 February 1782. Henry FREDERICK and Molly Sanderson, who writes her own consent. Molly is daughter of Joseph Sanderson, deceased. Sur. John Howard. Wit. George Laughlin. p. 36.

11 September 1787. John FREEMAN and Sarah Willis, dau. of
William and Susanna Willis who consent. Sur. Cuthbert Willis.
Wit. Samuel Alley. p. 35.

9 December 1806. Nathaniel FREEMAN and Lockey M. Angel, dau.
of William Angel who consents and states Lockey is over 21.
Judith Freeman consents for her son and says he is of age.
Sur. William Angel. Wit. Frederick Freeman, James Valentine,
Henry Drake. p. 36.

15 April 1806. John Francis FREIMON and Adelaide E. Delaplanche.
Sur. Francis Vanet who makes oath Adelaide is over 21. p. 36.

10 September 1795. Henry FRENCH and Nancy Carrel, who consents;
dau. of Thara? Graham who also consents. Sur. and Wit. Thomas
Nevil. Henry of the state of New Hampshire. p. 36.

2 December 1793. John FRIEND and Judith Cox. Sur. Edward
Cox. p. 36.

12 October 1807. Loammy FROST and Sarah Sneed. Sur. Jesse
Blackburn. p. 36.

11 April 1807. William FROST and Mary L. Coutts, orphan of
Reubin Coutts. Sur. Lewis Coutts. p. 36.

Before August 1692. Gill FUCQUE and Jane Eyres, dau. of Joseph
Eyres, deceased. Orphans Court, 1677-1739. p. 32.

24 September 1803. Alexander FULTON and Eliza B. Mayo, dau.
of William Mayo who consents. Sur. John G. Gamble. Wit. Ann
Randolph and Eliza Cordis. p. 36.

10 December 1807. Joshua FUQUA and Mary Tyre, who writes her
own consent. Sur. Henry Fuqua. Wit. Peter West. p. 36.

14 December 1785. Solomon FUSSEL and Sary Hutching, who
consents. Sur. Thomas Fussell. p. 36.

20 October 1785. Benjamin FUSSEL and Mrs. Sarah Matthews, who
consents. Sur. John Williams. Wit. James Childress. p. 36.

6 January 1787. John FUSSELL and Jane Williamson, dau. of
George Williamson, deceased. Sur. John Williamson, brother of
Jane, who certifies she is over 21, and is surety with John
Castlin. p. 36.

17 December 1792. William FUZZEL and Elizabeth Trueman, who
consent. Sur. Littlebury Royster. Wit. George Harwood.
p. 36.

14 May 1789. Albert GALLATIN and Sophia Allegre, who consents.
Sur. and Wit. Savary De Valcoulon. p. 37.

28 October 1790. Henry GARDNER and Patsy Green, who consents. Sur. William Breedlove. Wit. James Cummins. p. 37.

27 August 1791. Henry GARDNER and Catharine Bolton, who consents. Sur. and Wit. Matthias Conrad. p. 37.

9 December 1790. Absalom GARTHRIGHT and Martha Smith, of lawful age; dau. of William and Elizabeth Smith. Sur. Jesse Blackburn. Wit. Drury Wood and Mary Blackburn. p. 37.

23 December 1808. Anselmn GARTHRIGHT and Polly Garthright. Sur. James Binford who makes oath Polly is over 21. p. 37.

24 February 1788. John GARTHRIGHT and Sarah Woodfin, dau. of John James Woodfin who consents and is surety. p. 37.

13 September 1793. Joseph GARTHRIGHT and Phobe Hallock, who consents. Sur. Thomas Garthright. Wit. Samuel Goode. p. 37.

8 September 1800. Samuel G. GARTHRIGHT and Jemimah Baker. Sur. Tarpley Garthright. p. 37.

28 April 1807. Tarpley GARTHRIGHT and Elizabeth Garthright, widow. Sur. Jackson Frayser. p. 37.

6 May 1803. William GARTHRIGHT and Elizabeth Dumass. Sur. James Woodfin who makes oath Elizabeth is over 21. p. 37.

14 October 1796. Obediah GATHRIGHT and Jane Gathright, who consents. Sur. Daniel Woodson. Wit. John Miller and William Worsham. p. 37.

14 September 1796. Samuel GATHRIGHT and Mary Eubank, of lawful age. Sur. and Wit. John Eubank. p. 37.

7 August 1788. Denis GAUTIER and Frances Saunderson, who consents. Sur. Francis Trouin. p. 37.

26 November 1792. Daniel GAY and Mary Ray, who consents. Sur. Francis Pearce. Wit. Thomas Wilkins. p. 37.

Before 5 October 1725. Gilbert GEE and Katharine Roberts, widow of John Roberts. Orphans Court, 1677-1739. p. 53.

27 April 1793. Thomas GENNET and Jenny Alley. Sur. Peter Price. Wit. William, John, and Mary Alley. p. 37.

17 July 1789. David GEOINE and Clawey Webb, who consents. Sur. John Geoine who makes oath Clawey is over 21. Wit. William Ellis, Anne Going, Lain I. Johnson. p. 38.

22 October 1806. Alexander GEORGE and Polly Gathright. Sur. Christian Allen. p. 38.

18 June 1790. Edward GEORGE and Maria Stephens, dau. of Samuel Stevens who consents. Sur. George Robinson. Wit. Robert Pleasants, Thomas Thompson. p. 38.

23 November 1784. Reuben GEORGE and Betsey Sharp. Sur. Richard Sharp. p. 38.

18 September 1786. William GEORGE and Nancy Garthright, dau. of William Garthright who consents and is surety. p. 38.

11 July 1808. Theodore Alexander GERARD and Martha Atkinson, dau. of John Atkinson who is surety. p. 38.

30 January 1795. Knowles GILES and Lucy Bullington, of lawful age; dau. of Sarah Bullington. Sur. Austin Talman. Wit. Thomas Clopton and Drury Wood. p. 38.

By 9 March 1683. William GILES and Bethenia Knowles, dau. of Capt. John Knowles, deceased. Deeds, Wills, etc., 1677-1692. p. 232.

24 April 1788. Charles GILL and Virlynch Branch. Sur. William Coulter. p. 38.

18 February 1808. Martin GILLET and Eliza E. Adair, ward of Daniel W. Lacknider who consents and is surety. Mary Lalend? mother of Eliza, also consents. p. 38.

12 November 1789. Thomas GILLIAT and Mary Scott, dau. of Thomas Scott who consents. Sur. John Wilson. Wit. John Robinson, Jr., and W. P. Jones. p. 38.

13 November 1799. Dudley GILMAN and Polley Ford, dau. of Samuel Ford who is surety. p. 38.

1 January 1790. Thomas GINNINGS and Susanna Griffin, who consents. Sur. Obediah Griffin. Wit. Pierce Griffin and Cullen Jones. p. 38.

28 September 1798. Cornelius GLENN and Catharine Bridgwater, of lawful age; dau. of Nathaniel Bridgwater. Sur. Zachariah Bridgwater. p. 38.

24 December 1794. John GLENN and Susanna Smith, who consents. Sur. and Wit. Drury Wood. p. 38.

5 July 1790. William GLENN and Susanna Cornet, who consents. Sur. Francis Shepperson. Wit. W. Allen and Allen Cornet. p. 38.

9 September 1800. Matthew GLINN and Elizabeth Tinsley. Sur. Hezekiah Jennings who makes oath Elizabeth is over 21. p. 39.

26 May 1791. Peter GLOVACRE and Anne Moore, widow, who consents. Sur. Ballezar Dorisch. Wit. Nancy Lanson, Lain I. Johnson. p. 38.

14 September 1808. Thomas GLOVER and Mary Allen. Sur. John Brooks who makes oath Mary is over 21. p. 39.

3 July 1786. John GLYNN and Mary Taylor Geoghegan, dau. of Anthony Geoghegan who consents and is surety. p. 39.

25 May 1798. Isham GODDIN and Elizabeth Harwood, dau. of Elisha Harwood who consents. Sur. John Courtney. p. 39.

14 August 1782. George GODFREY and Elizabeth Adams, of lawful age. Sur. and Wit. Charles Mathews. p. 39.

1 March 1791. Benjamin GOODE and Mary Garthright, dau. of Samuel Garthright who consents. Sur. Joseph Pleasants. Wit. Benjamin and William Garthright. p. 39.

29 January 1791. Daniel GOODE and Susanna Johnson, dau. of Robert Johnson who consents. Daniel son of John Goode who consents. Sur. William Robertson. Wit. Joseph Pleasants. p. 39.

5 November 1793. John GOODE and Fanny Childress, who consents. Sur. William Robertson. Wit. Thomas Clarke and Edward Goode. p. 39.

19 February 1806. John GOODE and Phobe Garthright, widow of Joseph Garthright. Sur. John Lindsey. p. 39.

21 January 1794. Joseph GOODE and Ann Thomas Gay. Sur. Charles Gay. p. 39.

19 February 1803. Samuel GOODE and Mary Woodfin, dau. of John James Woodfin. Sur. William Garthright who makes oath Mary is over 21. p. 39.

7 June 1798. William GOODWIN and Sarah Thornton. Sur. Richard Denny. p. 39.

14 March 1783. William GOODWYN and Elizabeth Pinchback, of lawful age. Sur. John Roper. p. 39.

13 September 1792. James GORDON and Ann Mewes, who consents. Sur. Jonathan Hutchins. Wit. Ansel George, John Gordon, Sherod Foard. p. 39.

14 May 1807. James GORDEN and Mrs. Mary Tucker, widow. Sur. Joshua West. p. 39.

20 January 1807. James H. GORDON and Maria R. Webb, orphan of George Webb. John D. Blair, guardian of Maria, consents for her. Sur. William Kendall Lee. Wit. William Radford and James Blair. p. 39.

9 April 1783. John GORDON and Agness Bridgwater. Sur. Robert Sneed. Wit. William Whitlock. p. 40.

16 December 1784. Obediah GORDON and Elizabeth Gadberry, who consents. Sur. John Gordon. Wit. Thomas and Prudence Gadberry. p. 40.

14 March 1786. Thomas GORDON and Mary Hughes, who consents. Sur. Edward Nevill. p. 40.

21 March 1798. Hugh GRAHAM and Nancy Freeman. Sur. Joshua West. p. 40.

16 June 1806. Joseph GRANT and Charity Wyse, of the City of Richmond. Sur. John Craddock who makes oath Charity is over 21. p. 40.

9 March 1789. Michael GRANTLAND and Christian Pinchback, sister of Thomas Pinchback who consents and is surety. Wit. Elizabeth Goodwin. p. 40.

19 August 1783. Francis GRAVES and Martha Johnson, dau. of William Johnson. Sur. John Stockdell. Wit. Michael Johnson, I. Shackelford, Samuel Patteson. p. 40.

3 November 1789. John GREEN and Mary Craddock, dau. of Sary Craddock who consents. Sur. John Craddock. Wit. Thomas Pinchback. p. 40.

7 July 1806. John GREEN and Judith Rice, his ward. Sur. James Taylor. p. 40.

Before 2 October 1693. Robert GREEN and Elinor Burroughs, widow of Bartholemew Burroughs. Orphans Court, 1677-1739. p. 34.

23 April 1787. William GREEN and Elizabeth Williams. Sur. and Wit. Elisha Williams, brother of Elizabeth who states she is over 21. p. 40.

23 April 1793. William GREEN and Mary Rice Bennett, dau. of Richard Bennett who consents. Sur. John Craddock. Wit. Richard Watkins. p. 40.

31 December 1789. John GREENHOW and Katherine Voss, dau. of Edward Voss who consents. Sur. Robert Greenhow. Wit. Thomas D Harris. p. 40.

11 April 1792. John GREENHOW and Elizabeth Duval. Sur. Samuel Greenhow. Wit. Jeremiah Strother. p. 40.

26 June 1786. Robert GREENHOW and Ann Wills, dau. of Elias Wills who consents and is surety. p. 40.

21 December 1808. Michael GRETTER and Joanna Hewlett. Sur. William McEnery. p. 40.

9 March 1807. Abner GRIFFIN and Polly Robertson, who consents. Sur. Cornelius Glenn who makes oath Polly is over 21. p. 41.

8 November 1802. James GRIFFIN and Sarah Thorp, dau. of William Thorp who is surety. p. 41.

19 July 1792. Obadiah Griffin and Polley Thorp, dau. of Thomas Thorp who consents. Sur. John Thorp. Wit. Watson Talmon. p. 41.

26 January 1791. Pierce GRIFFIN and Juda Allen, of lawful age; dau. of James Allen, Sr.. Sur. Obediah Griffing. Wit. James Allen, Jr. p. 41.

27 November 1794. William GRIFFIN and Susanna Kelly. Sur. George Kelly. p. 41

13 October 1798. William GRIFFIN and Nancy Woolbanks, of lawful age. Sur. James Grinstead. Wit. William Price. p. 41.

31 July 1807. Benjamin GRIFFITH and Mary Gantz, dau. of John F. Gantz who is surety. p. 41.

4 November 1785. Joseph GRIFFITH and Mrs. Patsey McMeecan, who consents. Sur. William Barker. Wit. Matthew Hobson. p. 41.

Before 20 August 1700. Robert GRIGG and Tabitha Gower, orphan of Abell Gower. Orphans Court, 1677-1739. p. 43.

17 December 1799. James GRINSTEAD and Lydia Holoway, widow. Sur. William Thorp. Wit. Andrew Stevenson. p. 41.

2 February 1801. John GRINSTEAD and Elizabeth Southworth. Watson Patman, guardian of Elizabeth, consents and is surety. p. 41.

25 March 1803. Philip GRINSTEAD and Lucy Hooker. Sur. Samuel Evans who makes oath Lucy is over 21 and a resident of the City of Richmond. p. 41.

19 March 1799. Anderson GRUBBS and Nancy Hall. Sur. Josiah Mosby. p. 41.

26 March 1801. David S. GRYMES and Susanna Pratt, widow. Sur. Bennett McAllister who makes oath David is over 21, and Susanna a resident of the City of Richmond. p. 41.

2 July 1784. John GUN and Sally Schearer. Sur. William Moseley. p. 41.

8 June 1790. John GUNN and Nancy Forde. Sur. Samuel Ford. Wit. G. Laughlin. p. 41.

3 May 1787. John HALES and Catherine White, who consents. Sur. William Carter. Wit. Joanna White, J------ White, Samuel Hales. p. 43.

31 January 1789. Benjamin HALEY and Anney Spurr, who consents. Sur. Thomas Johnson. Wit. William Spurr and Charles Wright. p. 43.

24 August 1808. Joseph HALL and Elizabeth Waid, who consents.
Sur. William Meredith. James P. Wilsford makes oath Elizabeth
is over 21. p. 43.

10 May 1787. William HALL and Maryann Mattox, widow of William
Mattox. Sur. Robert C. Fariss. Wit. Joshua Morris. p. 43.

Before 5 October 1725. James HAMBLETON and Martha Moseby, widow
of John Moseby. Orphans Court, 1677-1739. p. 54.

27 May 1797. John HAMILL and Aggy Deane, of lawful age. Sur.
and Wit. John Cocke. p. 43.

13 February 1796. Thomas HAMLET and Sally Parker. Sur. Jephta
Parker. p. 43.

June 1696. Stephen HAMLIN and Mary Elam. Sur. Richard Cocke,
Jr. Deeds, Wills, etc., 1688-1697. p. 631.

14 July 1797. Rowland HAMPTON and Elizabeth Jordan, of lawful
age. Sur. and Wit. Pearin Redford. p. 43.

8 September 1802. William HAMPTON and Elizabeth Williams. Sur.
Joseph Foster who makes oath William is over 21. Samuel William
makes oath Elizabeth is over 21. p. 43.

23 April 1808. Michael W. HANCOCK and Sophia Scott, who consents.
Sur. Thomas Gilliat. p. 43.

5 April 1700. Samuel HANCOCK and Joane Hancock. Deeds, Wills,
etc., 1697-1704. p. 220.

11 April 1793. Thomas HARDY and Salley Patten. Sur. Gershoin
Patten. p. 43.

21 January 1801. John HARLAN and Elizabeth Liggon, dau. of John
Liggon who is surety. p. 43.

21 February 1792. John HARLOW and Mary Gentry, who consents.
Sur. Meredith Childress. Wit. Richard Loving and John ----- p. 43.

21 September 1792. John HARLOW and Milley Going. Agness Goyne
consents; no relationship stated. Sur. David Going. Wit.
John Geoine. p. 43.

31 May 1792. John HARPER and Ursula Sharp, who consents. Sur.
Samuel Byrns. Wit. Nancy and Isaac Sharp. p. 44.

29 December 1800. William HARPER and Betsey Hewlett, dau. of
William Hewlett who is surety. p. 44.

20 June 1787. Joseph HARREL and Patsey Emery, widow, of lawful
age. Sur. John McAlister. Wit. Thomas and John Miller. p. 44.

11 June 1790. Eldridge HARRIS and Celia Voss. Sur. George
Laughlin. p. 44.

4 September 1807. George D. HARRIS and Elizabeth Cee, widow. Sur. Cyrus Jones. p. 44.

27 August 1795. John HARRIS and Mary Shearley, who consents. Sur. David Blackwell. Wit. Stephen Haynes. p. 44.

26 June 1695. Peter HARRIS and Mary Smith. Deeds, Wills, etc., 1688-1697. p. 604.

25 January 1697. Timothy HARRIS and Elizabeth Womack. Deeds, etc., 1697-1699. p. 96.

14 October 1808. Jacob HARRISON and Elizabeth Royster. Sur. John H. Strobia. p. 44.

15 September 1788. George HARWOOD and Rebecca Winston, who consents. Sur. George Winston. Wit. Benjamin Haley, Edm'd. Winston, Pleasant Winston. p. 44.

25 December 1792. James HARWOOD and Fanny Boles, who consents. Sur. John Brown. Wit. Pleasant Hazlewood. p. 44.

28 July 1801. Pleasant HARWOOD and Elizabeth Carter. Sur. William Burton. John Carter makes oath Elizabeth is over 21. p. 44.

14 June 1694. Samuel HARWOOD and Temperance Cook. Deeds, Wills, etc., 1688-1697. p. 552.

2 June 1801. Samuel HARWOOD and Anne Farrar. Sur. Josiah Bingham. Pleasant Harwood makes oath Samuel, his brother, is over 21. p. 44.

30 May 1790. Thomas HARWOOD and Faney Baley, who consents. Sur. Elisha Harwood. Wit. Nat. Childers, F. L. Claiborne. p. 44.

29 August 1782. William HARWOOD and Susanna Spears. Robert Spears consents; no relationship stated. Sur. and Wit. George Harwood. p. 44.

28 April 1801. Williamson HARWOOD and Susannah Allen, dau. of Richard Allen who is surety. Peter Bailey makes oath Williamson is over 21. p. 44.

Between 1688-1689. Edward HASKINS and Martha Jones. Deeds, Wills, etc., 1688-1697. p. 97.

25 September 1682. William HATCHER and daughter of John Burton. Deeds, Wills, etc., 1677-1692. p. 225.

21 August 1793. William HAWES and Elizabeth Faris, of lawful age; dau. of Sarah Faris. Sur. Thomas Puryear. Wit. David Going, Susannah Faris, John Faris, Martha Roper. p. 44.

9 April 1794. John HAWKINS and Lucy Smith, dau. of Obediah Smith who consents. Sur. William Burton. Wit. Daniel Burton. p. 44.

1 October 1787. Harden HAYNES and Edith Ellis, dau. of Joseph Ellis who consents. Sur. Henry Ellis. Wit. Henry Puryear. p. 45.

12 December 1806. Samuel HAYWOOD and Martha Franklin, dau. of Elisha Franklin who consents. Sur. Herman G. Sneed. Wit. E. I. Clopton. p. 45.

17 August 1798. Pleasant HAZLEWOOD and Rhody Tyler. Sur. Shelton Tyler. p. 45.

12 November 1807. William HAZLEWOOD and Sally Jackson, dau. of Reuben Jackson who is surety. p. 45.

1 January 1789. John HEATH and Elizabeth Bethel, who consents. Sur. William Pinchback. Wit. John Dean, Peter Leneve, James Coryell, Henry --------. p. 45.

31 March 1806. William HENDERSON and Paky Bailey, dau. of John Bailey who is surety. p. 45.

2 January 1793. Robert HENDREN and Molley Bridgwater. Sur. James Roberts. p. 45.

13 April 1803. Robert HENDREN and Martha Williams. Sur. Andrew Williams, brother of Martha, who makes oath she is over 21. p. 45.

6 May 1801. Leonard HENLEY and Rebecca P. Miller, dau. of Edward Miller who consents. Sur. John Gathright. Wit. John J. Dickinson. p. 45.

20 November 1807. Samuel HENRY and Martha Spurlock. Sur. Nathaniel White. Samuel Liggan makes oath Martha is over 21. p. 45.

10 September 1789. William HERBERT and Sally Johnson, dau. of Thomas Johnson, Sr. who consents. Sur. John Williamson. Wit. J. Rose and John Green. p. 45.

9 September 1695. John HESTER and Mary Worsham. Deeds, Wills, etc., 1688-1697. p. 604.

10 November 1787. Harry HETH and Nancy Haire. Sur. Philip Southall. p. 45.

2 April 1694. Henry HILL and Rosemond Webster. Sur. Capt. Peter Field. Deeds, Wills, etc., 1688-1697. p. 467.

19 November 1807. Josiah HILL and Susannah H. Cobbs. David Cobbs, guardian of Susannah, consents for her. Sur. George White. Wit. Elisha White. p. 45.

24 December 1806. Benjamin HILLIARD and Polly Winston Harwood. Sur. George Harwood. p. 45.

20 March 1799. Jesse HIX and Polley Buckner, of lawful age. Sur. Aylett Buckner. Wit. William Price. p. 45.

25 November 1785. John HIX and Sarah Grubb, dau. of John Grubb who consents. Sur. Cornelius Tolar. p. 45.

18 May 1701. Robert HIX and Kathrine (Ruth) Ragsdaile. Sur. Capt. William Farrar. Deeds, Wills, etc., 1697-1704. p. 243.

18 April 1795. Samuel HOBSON and Patsey Frayser, of lawful age; dau. of William Frayser. Sur. Joseph Pleasants. Wit. Stephen Childrey. p. 46.

23 October 1784. James HODGES and Sarah Townley, dau. of Martha Townley who consents. Sur. John Vaden. p. 46.

27 January 1797. James HOGG and Milly Holmes. Sur. William Holmes. Wit. Wilson Allen. p. 46.

17 February 1791. Samuel HOGG and Susanna Bowles, of lawful age. Samuel son of Micajah Hogg. Sur. Abselem Melton. Wit. William Grinstead, Mary Grinstead, Benjamin Howard. p. 46.

29 December 1785. James HOLLINGS and Rasilla Derrom. Sur. William Barret. p. 46.

14 November 1799. David HOLLOWAY and Julia Lee Dove, widow, who consents. Sur. and Wit. Obediah Gathright. p. 46.

31 October 1797. James HOLLOWAY and Judith Staples, dau. of William Staples who is surety. p. 46.

7 March 1782. Nathaniel HOLLOWAY and Mary Eubank. Sur. James Waddill. p. 46.

5 March 1798. Robert HOLLOWAY and Martha White. Henry and Elizabeth White consent; no relationship stated. Sur. Joseph White and Austin Glazebrook. p. 46.

24 October 1798. Henry HOLMAN and Elizabeth DuVal. Henry son of Nathaniel Holman. Sur. Jos. DuVal. Wit. Abraham -----, James Mann. p. 46.

21 December 1797. John HOLMAN and Frances Chockley, who consents. Sur. Daniel Burton. p. 46.

3 February 1798. Benjamin HOLMS and Anne Dollard, widow. Sur. Thomas Bethel. p. 46.

15 November 1786. Thomas HOLTON and Regina Dunnaberry. Sur. Alexander Quarrier who consents for Regina and states she is under age. p. 46.

6 February 1786. Thomas HOOD and Elizabeth Branch Bailey. Joseph Bailey, guardian of Elizabeth, consents for her and is surety. Wit. William Whitlock. p. 46.

16 February 1803. James HOOKER and Anne Sneed, dau. of Charles Sneed who is surety. p. 46.

25 November 1807. William HOOMER, Jr. and Susanna Tucker. Sur. Gideon Bosher. p. 46.

27 January 1790. James HOOPER and Elizabeth Franklin, of lawful age. Sur. William Thorp. Wit. Elijah Franklin. p. 46.

30 July 1807. James HOOPER and Elizabeth Williams, widow. Sur. Richard Bennett. p. 46.

27 October 1808. Jeremiah HOOPER and Mary Bowles. Sur. John Magahee who makes oath Mary is over 21. p. 46.

29 September 1795. Peary HOOPER and Agness Freeman, of lawful age; dau. of Elizabeth Freeman. Sur. and Wit. Daniel Ockerman. p. 47.

September 1704. Benjamin HORNER and Mary Ruck. Deeds, Wills, etc., 1697-1704. p. 450.

6 January 1789. Joseph HOUSE and Sarah Jones, of lawful age; dau. of Mary Jones. Sur. Joseph Leplan and John Crawford. Wit. Robbin Martin and Alecy Chappel. p. 47.

26 February 1807. Francis HOWARD and Margaret Scherer. John Adams, guardian of Margaret, consents for her. Sur. William Mann. Wit. Ph. Rogers and Samuel G. Adams. p. 47.

27 January 1803. William Lewis HOWARD and Frances Woolbanks. Sur. Pierce Griffing who makes oath Frances is over 21. p. 47.

17 January 1801. Wilkinson HOWD and Elizabeth Rogers, dau. of John Rogers, deceased, and Martha Pearman. Luke Fowler, guardian of Elizabeth, consents for her. Sur. Kirkland Rogers. Wit. Wyatt Walker and Elizabeth Black. p. 47.

4 February 1782. John HOWELL and William Gadberry. Sur. William Gadberry. Note: This is an error. Clerk wrote in surety's name instead of bride. p. 47.

31 August 1791. Haritage HOWERTON and Nancy Hazlewood. Sur. Joshua Hazlewood. p. 47.

5 October 1796. James HOWERTON and Sarah Cootes, dau. of William Cootes who consents. Sur. James Grinstead. p. 47.

15 January 1789. James HOWEY and Catharine Short, dau. of
Margaret Atkinson who certifies Catharine is over 21. Sur.
John Atkinson. Wit. Fisher Bennett and John Kemp. p. 47.

12 November 1792. Epaphroditus HOWLE and Polley Chandler, who
consents. Sur. Isaac Ramsbottom who certifies Polly is over
21. Wit. James Bisset and Tho. Kelly. p. 47.

22 January 1693. Benjamin HUDSON and Elizabeth Skipp. Sur.
James Cocke. Deeds, Wills,etc., 1688-1697. p. 467.

29 September 1791. Charles HUDSON and Mary Price, dau. of
Barret Price who consents. Sur. William Price. Wit. Elisha
Price. p. 47.

2 January 1785. John HUDSON and Nancy Williams. Thomas
Childrey, guardian of Nancy, consents for her. Sur. John
Williams. p. 47.

Before 5 October 1725. Peter HUDSON and Martha Pride, widow
of Halcot Pride. Orphans Court, 1677-1739. p. 54.

Between 1688-1689. Ralph HUDSPETH and Margaret Eyres. Deeds,
Wills, etc., 1688-1697. p. 97.

25 August 1788. Benjamin HUGHES and Mary Johnson. John Miller,
guardian of Mary, consents for her and is surety. Wit. William
Price, Jr. p. 47.

1 November 1787. Emmery HUGHES and Elizabeth Woodcock, of lawful
age; dau. of Isaac Woodcock, dec'd. and Lucy Woodcock. Sur.
Richard Burnett. Wit. Samuel Coleman and William Woodcock.
p. 47.

29 August 1789. William HUGHES and Milley Holman, dau. of
Nathaniel Holman who consents. Sur. Thomas Bowles. Wit.
John Strong. p. 48.

1 March 1782. John HULL and Anne Strachan, dau. of Peter Strachan
who consents. Sur. John Barret. John Hull of Northumberland
County. p. 48.

3 January 1803. William HUMBER and Charlotte Matilda Hodgson.
Sur. William Hodgson. William Humber of Goochland County.
p. 48.

19 March 1788. Harrison HUMPHREY and Sarah Harlow, who consents.
Sur. John Geoine. Wit. David Geoine. p. 48.

8 March 1797. Nelson HUNDLEY and Ann Wichen, of lawful age. Sur.
Elisha Archer. Note: Bond reads Ann, consent reads Mary and is
signed by Ann Wichen, mother. p. 48.

24 December 1794. Ichabod HUNTER and Elizabeth Seldon. Sur.
John Kerr. p. 48.

18 September 1788. John HUVER and Abathsheba Miller, who consents.
William Miller, father of Abathsheba, also consents and is surety.
Wit. Sary Miller, William Miller, Jr., John Price, Elisha Mill.
p. 48.

22 January 1791. Robert HYDE and Ann East, widow, who consents.
Sur. Thomas Howell. Wit. Ann Howell. p. 48.

5 March 1788. Francis HYLAND and Rebecca Cocke, who consents.
Sur. John Burris. Wit. Charles Conway. p. 48.

13 February 1808. Thomas HYLAND and Milored Rogers, widow.
Sur. Benjamin Mitchell. p. 48.

28 February 1793. Charles IRBY and Phebe Childers, dau. of
John Childers who consents. Sur. Absalom Lawrence. Wit. John
Edwards. p. 49.

28 October 1693. Josua IRBY and Elizabeth Ludson. Sur. Thomas
Chamberlayne. Deeds, Wills, etc., 1688-1697. p. 467.

About 1686. William IRBY, Jr. and Elizabeth Mascall, wid. of
Richard Mascall. William of Charles City County. Deeds, Wills,
etc., 1688-1697. p. 443.

21 May 1806. Holly JACKSON and Betty Skinner, a free black
woman, emancipated by William Randolph. Richard Adams certifies
Holly Jackson bought his freedom. p. 51.

28 January 1791. Joseph JACKSON and Mary E. Carter, dau. of
William Carter, Sr. who consents. Sur. James Wray. p. 51.

4 November 1784. Reuben JACKSON and Frances West. Sur. James
Valentine. p. 51.

18 March 1808. Toba JACKSON and Patt, a black woman. Sur.
William Dawson. p. 51.

24 August 1787. Toby JACKSON and Rebekah Jackson. Sur. John
Courtney. Wit. Benjamin Pollard. p. 51.

4 February 1786. Henry JAMAR and Jane Gateby, who consents.
Sur. Simon Murray. Wit. Jaine Gateby and John Bradish. Both
Henry and Jane residents of the City of Richmond. p. 51.

20 December 1788. Edmund JAMES and Susanna Sheppard, dau. of
Benjamin Sheppard who consents. Sur. Philip Sheppard. Wit.
John M. Sheppard. p. 51.

Before 5 October 1725. Francis JAMES and Mary Good, widow
of John Good. Orphans Court, 1677-1739. p. 54.

7 October 1808. Lightfoot JANNEY and Eliza Heth, who consents. Bartlett Burton makes oath Eliza is over 21. Sur. John Sheppard. Wit. Edu. Watkins and Ro. W. Christian. p. 51.

11 February 1806. William JARVIS and Frances Francis, widow of John Francis. Sur. William Priddy. p. 51.

21 July 1792. Moses JEFFERSON and Ann West, who consents. Sur. James Drummond. Wit. Margartt Drummond and John Cunliffe. p. 51.

20 November 1697. Thomas JEFFERSON and Mary Field, dau. of Peter Field. Deeds, etc., 1697-1699. p. 96.

5 January 1797. Joshua JENINGS and Nancy Morris, of lawful age. Sur. and Wit. Robert Morris. p. 51.

8 January 1802. Banjamin JENKINS and Sally West. Sur. Thomas Kersey. p. 51.

4 October 1802. David JENKINS and Frances Priddy. Sur. Benjamin Jenkins. p. 51.

11 January 1802. David JENNINGS and Frances Howerton, dau. of Thomas Howerton who consents and is surety. Jesse Jennings, father of David, consents for him. p. 52.

1 January 1794. Henry JENNINGS and Elizabeth Morriss, who consents. Elizabeth is daughter of Elizabeth Morriss. Sur. Jesse Jennings. Wit. Robert Morriss. p. 51.

22 December 1799. Samuel JENNINGS and Nancy Britain, dau. of Samuel Britain who is surety with Jesse Jennings, father of Samuel Jennings. p. 51.

5 April 1792. Nicholas JESSE and Salley Britain. Sur. Samuel Britain. Wit. Nathaniel Sheppard. p. 52.

27 November 1801. Archibald JOHNSON and Nancy Foster. Sur. John Foster who makes oath both are over 21. p. 52.

27 November 1789. Austin JOHNSON and Mildred Goode. Sur. William Robinson. p. 52.

19 May 1785. Benjamin JOHNSON and Mary Lenley. Sur. Leonard Henley. Note: Name of surety is also spelled Lenley in bond but signed Henley. p. 52.

28 March 1796. Benjamin JOHNSON and Mary Robertson, who consents. Sur. Benjamin Robertson. Wit. John Goode, William -----. p. 52.

27 September 1806. Chapman JOHNSON and Mary Ann Nicholson. Charles Copland, guardian of Mary Ann, consents for her. Sur. John H. Brown. Wit. P. Copland. p. 52.

29 August 1795. Charles JOHNSON and Susanna Nelson, of lawful age. Sur. James Moore. Wit. Wilson Allen, Jacob Lewis, James Jones. p. 52.

9 November 1802. David JOHNSON and Susanna McAllister, dau. of John McAllister who is surety. p. 52.

Between 1688-1689. John JOHNSON and Michall Harris. Deeds, Wills, etc., 1688-1697. p. 97.

17 February 1785. Levi JOHNSON and Kitchora Bowman. Sur. John Scott. p. 52.

21 October 1805. Reuben JOHNSON and Ann Reas. Sur. James Reas. p. 52.

11 March 1788. Thomas JOHNSON and Anne Lankford, who consents. Sur. Samuel Gawlin. Wit. Samuel Cooling and John Martin. p. 52.

3 January 1801. Thomas JOHNSON and Elizabeth Robinson, dau. of Mary Ann Robinson who consents. Sur. Nathaniel Robinson. Wit. William Murray. p. 52.

18 July 1806. Cornelius JOHNSTON and Elizabeth Cowley, dau. of Robert Cowley who is surety. Wilson Allen makes oath Cornelius is free born. p. 52.

1 January 1793. Henry C. JOHNSTON and Molley Gill, who consents. Sur. Anthony Barrow. Wit. Henry Tabb. p. 52.

10 December 1796. Robert JOHNSTON, Jr. and Elizabeth McCaw. Sur. James Drew McCaw. Elizabeth of the City of Richmond. p. 53.

2 July 1798. Robert JOHNSTON and Salley Evans, of lawful age; widow of Thomas Evans. Sur. Archibald Taylor. Wit. John Edwards. p. 52.

1 December 1790. Alexander JONES and Mary Ann Winston. Sur. Thomas Prosser. p. 53.

8 August 1798. Benjamin JONES and Polly Weymouth, of lawful age. Sur. Pleasant Hazlewood. Wit. Langsle Jones and Robert Sydnor. p. 53.

7 November 1801. Benjamin JONES and Susannah Parker, widow. Sur. John Parker. p. 53.

17 September 1807. Cyrus JONES and Judy Carter. Sur. George D. Harris who makes oath Judy is over 21. p. 53.

11 November 1795. James JONES and Susannah White, dau. of Henry White who is surety. p. 53.

19 August 1800. Jesse JONES and Mary Hazlewood, dau. of Joshua
Hazlewood who is surety. William Cresy, of Fluvanna County,
makes oath Jesse is over 21. p. 53.

Before 1680. John JONES and Anne Rowing, orphan of Henry Rowing.
Orphans Court, 1677-1739. p. 6.

7 May 1784. John JONES and Prudence Hazlewood, dau. of Mary
Hazlewood, of Hanover County, who consents. Wit. Hugh Mosely(?).
p. 53.

1 June 1797. John JONES and Tempy Scott. Sur. John Scott.
p. 53.

26 January 1795. Joshua JONES and Mary Richardson, who consents.
Sur. Ralph Graves. p. 53.

12 March 1807. Langston JONES and Rosanna T. Crump. Sur.
Francis Cornett who states he believes Rosanna to be over 21.
p. 53.

1688. Peter JONES and Mary Batte. Deeds, Wills, etc., 1688-1697.
p. 20.

12 October 1684. Philip JONES and Margarett Jones. Deeds, Wills,
etc., 1677-1692. p. 292.

24 October 1807. Reuben JONES and Sally Ailstock, dau. of
Joseph Ailstock who consents. Sur. Absalom Ailstock. Wit.
James Allen, Pleasant Thorp, Nancy M. Allen, Elizabeth Thorp.
p. 53.

15 February 1692. Richard JONES and Rachell Ragsdail. Sur.
Peter Jones. Deeds, Wills, etc., 1688-1697. p. 435.

13 December 1786. Richard JONES and Susannah Turner, who consents.
Sur. Thomas Ford. Wit. Obediah and Susaner Griffing. p. 53.

1 July 1808. Roger JONES and Mary Williams. Sur. George
Williamson. p. 53.

9 June 1791. Samuel JONES and Lucy Smith, dau. of Jesse Smith
who consents and is surety. p. 53.

13 February 1790. Joseph JOPLING and Susanna Bridgwater, dau.
of William Bridgwater, Sr. who consents and is surety. Wit.
William Bridgwater, Jr. and Jonathan Bridgwater. p. 53.

8 March 1787. Fleming JORDAN and Martha Warn. Sur. David
Royster. p. 54.

6 May 1808. Huddlesey JORDAN and Mary Hutson. Sur. John Hutson.
p. 53.

10 June 1808. Noble JORDAN and Fanny Garthright. Sur. Anselmn
Garthright who makes oath Fanny is over 21. p. 54.

18 January 1806. William JORDAN and Margaret Amey, of the City of Richmond. William is ward of John Burton, Jr. who consents for him. Sur. Christopher Drummond and David Logan who certifies Margaret is over 21. Wit. Jackson Hampton. p. 54.

22 January 1795. Robert JOUET and Alice Lewis, dau. of Benjamin Lewis who is surety. Robert of Albemarle County. Note: Bond written Jouet but signature is Jouitt. p. 53.

15 December 1807. John H. JUDE and Rhoda Cawthron. Sur. James Cawthorn who certifies Rhoda is over 21. p. 54.

19 September 1790. Francis JUHAN and Rebecca Woodward. Sur. James Hamilton who consents and certifies Rebecca is over 21, and is the daughter of his wife, Ann Hamilton, formerly Ann Woodward. p. 54.

4 August 1787. Henry KALEY and Mary Jones, who consents. John Howard, of the City of Richmond, certifies Mary is over 21, and an orphan. Sur. Henry Frederick. Wit. Charles Lewis. p. 55.

23 December 1808. Joseph KAY and Frances Miller. Sur. Thomas Gould who certifies Frances is over 21. p. 55.

8 April 1800. Nevin KEARNES and Henrietta Price, ward of Alexander Blackwood who is surety. Note: Bond written Kearnes, but signature is Karins. p. 55.

4 August 1788. Charles KEESEE and Rebecca Smith. Elizabeth Smith, guardian of Rebecca, consents for her; no relationship stated. Sur. Francis Pearce. Wit. Thomas Keesee and Samuel Norment. p. 55.

15 February 1808. John KEESEE and Lucy Brightwell, dau. of Sally and Reynolds Brightwell who consent. Lucy is of age. Sur. Robert Johnson. p. 55.

20 April 1790. Thomas KEESEE and Elizabeth Burton, who consents. Sur. Arthur Giles. Wit. Knowles Giles. p. 55.

19 March 1796. Thomas KEESEE and Polley Otey, who consents. Sur. Thomas Otey. Wit. Peter Sharp and Samuel Norment. p. 55.

30 December 1792. Austin KELLEY and Sarah White. Sur. Elias White. p. 55.

27 January 1798. Charles KELLEY and Rachel Bennett, widow. Sur. Edward Harper. Wit. William Richardson. p. 55.

13 March 1801. William KELLEY and Mary Glenn. Sur. Cornelius Glenn who makes oath Mary is over 21. p. 55.

27 May 1793. John KELLY and Katy Payne, who consents. Sur. and Wit. James Cawthorn and James Bisset. p. 55.

1 November 1795. John KELLY and Martha Blackburn, who consents.
Sur. and Wit. Roland Blackburn. p. 55.

31 March 1787. Vallentine KELLY and Frances Burton, who consents.
Sur. Benjamin Kelly and Littleberry Rountree. Wit. George
Kelly and William Cocke. p. 55.

Before 20 August 1706. Richard KENDALL and Orphan of Thomas
Shippy. Orphans Court, 1677-1739. p. 48.

11 February 1796. John KERSEY and Susannah Tyler, of lawful age.
Sur. and Wit. Samuel Tyler. p. 55.

14 February 1798. Thomas KERSEY and Sally Jones, of lawful age.
Sur. Absolem Jones. p. 55.

5 May 1790. George KESEE and Frances Price, of lawful age.
Sur. Samuel Norment. Wit. John Enroughty and Ann Heth. p. 55.

23 December 1789. Thomas KEYS and Aggy Harden, dau. of Jesse
Harden who consents. Sur. John Williams. Wit. Andrew Williams.
p. 55.

29 December 1797. Pitman KIDD and Agness Sharp, widow of
Richard Sharp. Sur. Robert Coleman. Wit. Susanna H. Bradley.
p. 55.

31 May 1806. Richard KIDD and Lucy Foster. Sur. Jonathan
Foster who makes oath Lucy is over 21. p. 55.

5 February 1808. William KIDD and Catharine Oliver. Sur. James
Kidd who makes oath Catharine is over 21. p. 55.

Before 5 October 1725. Alexander KILPATRICK and Elizabeth Martin,
widow of Philip Martin. Orphans Court, 1677-1739. p. 53.

17 January 1795. Alexander KING and Polly Allen. Sur. Edward
Harper. Wit. Peter Price, David Allen, T. Sydnor. p. 56.

4 November 1795. Edward KNOX and Mrs. Agness Snead. Sur. John
Rice. Wit. J. Blagrove. p. 56.

20 November 1798. John LACEY, Jr. and Polly Alley, of lawful
age; dau. of Elizabeth Alley. Sur. John Lacy. Wit. William
Richardson, Aminadab Miller, Shadrack Lacy. p. 57.

13 February 1799. William LACEY and Salley Curle. Sur. John
Broun. p. 57.

13 June 1795. Daniel LACY and Nancy Neale, of lawful age.
Sur. and Wit. Lewis Neal. p. 57.

12 September 1787. John LACY and Rhoda Morris. Robert Morris, brother of Rhoda, consents and is surety. Wit. Samuel Lacy and Samuel Moody. p. 57.

7 August 1801. Shadrick LACY and Jane Allen. Sur. Jeremiah Burton who makes oath Jane is over 21. p. 57.

8 February 1806. James G. LAIDLEY and Harriet Quarries, dau. of Alexander Quarries, of the City of Richmond, who is surety. p. 57.

27 September 1782. David LAMBERT and Sally Ege. Sur. Isaac Younghusband. p. 57.

26 January 1792. Meredith LAMBERTH and Elizabeth Price, who consents. Sur. Samuel Lankester. Wit. Patsey Lennard, John Williamson, Mary Williamson. p. 57.

11 December 1791. William LAMBERTH and Elizabeth Irving, dau. of Mary Irving who consents. Sur. Benjamin Walton. Wit. H. Owin and Meredith Lambert. p. 57.

12 December 1792. Samuel LANCASTER and Mary Williamson. Sur. William Williamson. Note: Bond written Lancaster, but signed Lankister. p. 57.

3 July 1792. Jasper LANE and Anne Mallory, who consents. Sur. Stephen Haynes. Wit. John Blunt and Thomas Marshil. p. 57.

9 January 1794. John LANKFORD and Darcus Green. Sur. Elijah Green. p. 57.

18 December 1798. Thomas LANKFORD and Elizabeth Carter Fleming, who consents. Sur. Jesse Payne. Wit. John Payne and Reuben George. p. 57.

19 September 1791. John LAPRADE and Nancy Henley, dau. of William Henley who consents. Sur. Jacob Woodson. Wit. William Alley and Isaac Peak. p. 57.

20 November 1807. Edward LARK and Deborah Bingham, dau. of Josiah Bingham who consents. Sur. John Lark. Wit. Oliver T. Crop. p. 57.

24 November 1789. John LARK and Nancy Bennett, dau. of James Bennett who consents and is surety. p. 57.

20 March 1787. Joseph LATIL and Lucy Randolph. Sur. Beverley Randolph. p. 57.

14 April 1787. Robert LAUGHLIN and Martha Williams, who consents. Sur. John Liggan. Wit. Elisha Williams, William Smith, Elizabeth Williams. Samuel Smith. p. 57.

29 June 1807. John LAURENCE and Patsey Binford. Sur. William Flesher. Thomas Childrey makes oath Patsey is over 21. p. 58.

22 June 1787. Samuel LAURENCE and Sarah Perkins, who consents. Sur. Philip Goff. Wit. Fisher Bennett, Ludwell Laning, Richard Bennett. p. 58.

24 December 1791. William LAWRENCE and Elizabeth Rawlings. Sur. George Laughlin. p. 58.

21 November 1789. John LAWSON and Sarah Franklin, who consents. Sur. John Martin. Wit. William Anderson and Marker Vanderwall. p. 58.

2 August 1784. Philip LAWSON and Elizabeth Tawler, dau. of Susannah Tawler. Sur. and Wit. John Stockdell. p. 58.

18 February 1804. Thomas LAYNE and Salley Kelley. Valentine Kelley, guardian of Salley, consents for her. Sur. Bernard Reynolds. Wit. Pen(?) Clark and Martin Smith. p. 58.

30 November 1795. Austin LEAKE and Lucy Sheppard, dau. of Banjamin Sheppard who consents. Sur. Austin Morris. Wit. W. Allen, Benjamin ------. Austin of Albemarle County. p. 58.

22 April 1789. Charles LEE and Susanna Rebecca Young Spencer, who consents. Sur. and Wit. Thomas Wharton. p. 58.

26 April 1794. Andrew LEIPER and Frances Trent, dau. of Peterfield Trent who consents and is surety. p. 58.

17 August 1807. Ludwell LENEVE and Mary Hubbard. Sur. James Hooper who certifies Mary is over 21. p. 58.

17 July 1798. John B. LENNARD and Mary Wood, of lawful age. Sur. Thomas Lennard. Wit. William Price. p. 58.

5 March 1788. Thomas LENNARD and Catherine Wood, of lawful age. Sur. John Price and Banjamin Lennard. Wit. Samuel Lennard. p. 58.

6 March 1784. John LENOX and Peggy Ayscough. Sur. James Slate. p. 58.

5 May 1787. John LENOX and Lucy Campbell, of lawful age. Sur. and Wit. Malry Adams. p. 58.

24 April 1788. John LESTER and Sarah Hudson, dau. of T. H. Hudson who consents. Sur. John Hague. p. 58.

8 October 1791. Daniel LEWIS and Joanna Scott. Sur. Francis Lewis. p. 58.

24 December 1793. Jesse LEWIS and Elizabeth McGhee, who consents. Sur. William Cluff. Wit. Joseph, John, and Susannah McGhee. p. 58.

13 March 1792. John LEWIS and Anna Franklin, who consents. Sur. Elijah Franklin. p. 58.

5 December 1783. Joseph LEWIS and Mary Curd, who consents. Sur. and Wit. Charles Lewis. p. 58.

1 March 1787. Pleasant LEWIS and Jemimah Owen, who consents. Sur. John Price. Wit. Nathaniel Lewis, Robert Price, William Johnson. p. 58.

22 September 1788. Samuel LIGGAN and Bathsheba Harwood, who consents. Sur. George Winston. Wit. Edm'd. Winston and Rebecca Harwood. p. 59.

Before 1 April 1681. Richard LIGGON and Mary Worsham, dau. of Elizabeth Epes, deceased. Deeds, Wills, etc., 1677-1692. p. 164.

2 February 1697. Thomas LIGGON and Elizabeth Worsham. Deeds, etc., 1697-1699. p. 96.

14 July 1787. William LIGGON and Fanny Mathews, dau. of Rachel Mathews who consents. Sur. Nathaniel Couzins who certifies Fanny is over 21. p. 59.

25 July 1800. William LIGGON and Peggy Whitis. Sur. John Whitis. p. 59.

Between 1688-1689. Hugh LIGON and Elizabeth Walthall. Deeds, Wills, etc., 1688-1697. p. 97.

8 March 1785. Joseph LIPLONG and Elizabeth Nailor. Sur. Erasmus Rountree. Wit. William Whitlock and Abraham -----. p. 59.

20 February 1786. Adam LITCHFORD and Elizabeth Dean, dau. of William Dean who consents and is surety. p. 59.

29 August 1785. Robert LITTLE and Susanna Jeffs, who consents. Sur. Joseph Butler. Wit. James Gayle. p. 59.

10 August 1782. William LITTLEPAGE and Susanna Smith. Peter Winston consents for Susanna; no relationship stated. Sur. Hobson Owen. Wit. William Winston. p. 59.

4 December 1801. Peter LIVESAY and Susanna McGhee, dau. of John McGhee of Hanover County who consents. Sur. Joseph McGee. Wit. Elizabeth Lewis. p. 59.

15 February 1692. Benjamin LOCKETT and Winifred Pride. Deeds, Wills, etc., 1688-1697. p. 435.

19 August 1792. Henry LOGWOOD and Sarah Glass, dau. of Sally Glass who consents. Sur. Jedediah Allen. Wit. Benjamin Haley. p. 59.

24 December 1785. William LOGWOOD and Jane Walker, dau. of Isabelle Walker who consents. Sur. Edward Friend, Jr. Wit. William Elliott and Edward Warren. p. 59.

14 November 1787. John LONG and Margaret Hoy. Sur. John Clark. Wit. Benjamin Pollard. p. 59.

8 June 1782. Alexander LOVE and Mrs. Isabella Sinclair. Sur. John Beckley. p. 60.

15 January 1697. John LOWRY and Elizabeth Worrell. Deeds, etc., 1697-1699. p. 96.

24 December 1800. Wilson LUCAS and Lydia Lucas, dau. of Samuel Lucas who is surety and makes oath Wilson is over 21. p. 60.

28 March 1808. Thomas W. LUMPKIN and Elizabeth I. Smith, dau. of William S. Smith who consents. Sur. Benjamin Mosby. Wit. William Lacy. p. 60.

9 January 1808. Peyton LYNCH and Nancy Montgomery. Robert McKim, guardian of Nancy, is surety. p. 60.

28 September 1792. Bennet McALISTER and Lucy Bennet. Sur. James Bennett. p. 66.

13 April 1803. Charles McALLISTER and Polly Perkins. Sur. Hundley Perkins. p. 66.

18 December 1806. John McBRIDE and Harriot Lee. Sur. William Kendall Lee who makes oath Harriot is over 21. p. 66.

24 October 1805. William McCABE and Jane Collins. Sur. H. Y. Dabney. p. 66.

24 December 1790. Robert McCARTNEY and Arriana Gunn, who consents. Sur. Fred. Argyle. p. 66.

16 February 1791. William McCOY and Anne Clarke, dau. of Susanna Clarke who consents. Sur. William Nicolson. Wit. Samuel Browning and James Hubank. p. 66.

21 May 1785. James McDANIEL and Sarah Mogaway, widow, who consents. Sur. Francis Edwards. Wit. William Whitlock and Joseph Mogaway. p. 66.

9 September 1793. John McINTIRE and Susanna Talley, who consents. Sur. William Todd. Wit. Arthur Mann. p. 67.

21 January 1795. Donald McKENZIE and Sally Carter Harrison.
Sur. Edmund Harrison. p. 67.

9 October 1800. Andrew McKIM and Sarah Roper, dau. of Benjamin
Roper, deceased. John Bradley, guardian of Sarah consents for
her. Sur. Robert Warinner. Wit. Edward Roper. p. 67.

27 August 1788. John McKIM and Elizabeth Graves, who consents.
Sur. John Courtney. Wit. Edward Davis and Edward Carroll.
p.67.

19 December 1807. John McKIM and Eliza Harriet Page, widow.
Sur. Levin Blake. p. 67.

26 December 1793. William McKIM and Betsey Elliott. Sur.
Thomas Elliott. p. 67.

27 December 1808. Jonathan McLAIN and Martha Matthews. Sur.
William Childrey. p. 67.

12 February 1806. John MacNAUGHT and Magdaline Flint, ward
of George Pickett, of the City of Richmond. Sur. George Pickett.
p. 67.

21 September 1807. Alexander McRAE and Annie D. Hayes, dau. of
John Hayes, deceased. Sur. James Greenhow. p. 67.

22 December 1783. William H. MACON and Hannah Selden, dau. of
Miles Selden who consents. Sur. D. Ragsdale. William of New
Kent County. p. 61.

15 December 1802. Wilson MADDOX and Susanna Ellis, dau. of
Thomas Ellis, deceased. Sur. Charles Ellis who makes oath
Wilson is over 21. p. 61.

11 September 1787. Henry MADEIRASS and Nancy Wright. Samuel
Arnold, guardian of Nancy, consents for her and is surety. Nancy
is daughter of Henry Wright, deceased. Wit. John Price. p. 61.

23 April 1785. Joseph MALCOMB and Polly Lewis, dau. of Mary Lewis
who consents. Sur. and Wit. Nobel Jordan. p. 61.

1 December 1784. James MANN and Ann Sledd, who consents. Sur.
Daniel Burton. p. 61.

12 October 1787. William MANN and Dorithea Hutchins, of lawful
age. Sur. and Wit. John Kautzmann. p. 61.

8 January 1789. William MANN and Martha Lewis, of lawful age.
Martha is daughter of Mary Lewis. Sur. Thomas James. Wit. John
Burton. p. 61.

8 September 1798. Myer MARKS and Mrs. Sarah White. Sur. John
Degarnatt. Wit. R. Chapman. p. 61.

2 November 1795. Francis F. MARRIOTT and Huldak Pasley, of
lawful age; dau. of Solomon Pasley. Sur. Sterling Greavitt.
Wit. William James. p. 61.

20 February 1787. Aron MARSH and Mary Bowes, who consents.
Sur. Thomas Bowes (alias Hogg). Wit. Joseph Dancer and Thomas
Frankling. p. 61.

Before 20 August 1706. Allaxander MARSHALL and Elizabeth Ligon.
Orphans Court, 1677-1739. p. 48.

19 May 1789. James H. MARSHALL and Mary Warrington, of lawful
age. Sur. Benjamin Sheppard. Wit. Thomas Bowles and Rebeker
N --------. p. 61.

1 January 1783. John MARSHALL and Mary W. Ambler, dau. of
Jaquelin Ambler. p. 61.

27 June 1788. William MARSHALL and Alice Adams, dau. of
Richard Adams who consents. Sur. and Wit. James Marshall.
p. 61.

23 December 1791. David MARTIN and Frances Tucker. Sur. James
Tucker. Wit. Nathaniel Sheppard. p. 61.

30 March 1786. John MARTIN and Elizabeth Russell, dau. of Thomas
Russell who consents. Sur. James Drummond. p. 61.

13 January 1790. John MARTIN and Martha Price. James Price
consents for Martha; no relationship stated. Sur. Elisha Price.
Wit. Edw. Goode. p. 61.

14 June 1791. John MARTIN and Mary Priddy, dau. of Henry Priddy
who consents. Sur. John Lark. Wit. James and John Priddy.
p. 61.

17 February 1806. Martin F. MARTIN and Lucy Clarke Williams,
dau. of Edward Williams who consents. Sur. Taylor Williams.
Wit. George Chesman and T. C. B. Sneed. Lucy of the City of
Richmond. p. 61.

21 July 1794. Robert MARTYR and Frances Lawson, who consents.
Sur. John Lawson who certifies Frances is over 21. Wit. Thomas
Morris and Jesse Sadler. p. 62.

4 January 1803. Theodorick MASSIE and Elizabeth Carlile. Sur.
Jonathan Moore. p. 62.

1689. Edward MATHEWS and Sarah Bishop. Deeds, Wills, etc.,
1688-1697. p. 97.

13 May 1783. Frederick MATHEY and Susanna Welch. Sur. Simon
Murray. Wit. William Whitlock. p. 62.

28 July 1803. Reuben MATTHEWS and Sally W. Lord, dau. of Robinson Lord who is surety and makes oath Reuben is over 21. p. 62.

7 June 1783. Sampson MATTHEWS and Catharine Parke, who consents. Sur. Samuel Coleman. Wit. William and Polly Coleman. p. 62.

22 January 1784. Thomas MATTHEWS and Elizabeth Goode. Sur. Benjamin Goode. Wit. Robert Watkins. p. 62.

9 October 1807. William MATTHEWS and Susanna Matthews. Sur. James Matthews who makes oath Susanna is over 21. p. 62.

17 February 1700. Joseph MATTOX and Mary Jefferson, wid. of Thomas Jefferson. Deeds, Wills, etc., 1697-1704. p. 243.

Before 20 August 1706. John MAXFIELD and Mary Newcomb, orphan of Thomas Newcomb. Orphans Court, 1677-1739. p. 47.

27 October 1808. Thomas MAXWELL and Nancy Jude, dau. of Frederick Jude who certifies Nancy is of lawful age. Sur. Turner N. Henley. Wit. Thomas and John Jude. p. 62.

1 September 1685. Francis MAYBERRY and Elizabeth Bevin, widow of William Bevin. Deeds, Wills, etc., 1677-1692. pp. 331, 389.

28 April 1808. Joseph H. MAYO and Elizabeth D. Blair, dau. of John D. Blair who consents. Sur. James Drew McCaw. p. 62.

8 September 1786. John MAYSON and Mrs. Nancy Keep. Sur. William Porter. Note: Bond written Mayson but signature is Mason. p. 62.

26 February 1789. David MEADE, Jr. and Elizabeth Randolph, dau. of Col. Richard Randolph. Sur. Richard Randolph. Wit. Edm. Randolph. p. 62.

7 October 1807. Stith MEADE and Prudence Watkins Blakey, dau. of Reuben and Mary Blakey who consent. Sur. Joseph Pinnell. Wit. Peter Plunket. p. 62.

27 July 1793. Richard MEDLEY and Patsey Hylliard, who consents. Sur. Dennis Hanlon. p. 62.

23 December 1807. David MELTON and Polly Lucas. Sur. George Melton who makes oath Polly is over 21. p. 62.

29 June 1789. Capt. William MEREDITH and Sally Lewis, dau. of Joseph Lewis who consents. Sur. William Lewis. p. 63.

14 September 1793. John MICHAUX and Salley Peck, who consents. Sur. Miles Bott. Wit. Michael Grantham. p. 63.

26 March 1787. Caleb MILLER and Nancy Williams, of lawful age. Sur. and Wit. John Price. p. 63.

8 March 1792. Edward MILLER and Mary Clarke. Sur. Nathaniel Staples. p. 63.

21 March 1801. Elijah MILLER and Hanna Ellis, dau. of Joseph Ellis who is surety. John Miller, father of Elijah, consents for him. Wit. Leonard Henley and John Gathright. p. 63.

11 September 1788. Elisha MILLER and Elizabeth Alley, dau. of Elizabeth Alley who consents. Sur. John Price. Wit. Calup Miller. p. 63.

14 October 1784. Francis MILLER and Ann Warriner. Sur. John Lynar. p. 63.

13 April 1784. John MILLER and Sarah Pond. Sur. Benjamin Philips. p. 63.

15 May 1799. John MILLER and Susanna Croxton, dau. of Thomas Croxton who is surety. p. 63.

26 May 1798. Melchicidec MILLER and Nancy Griffin, of lawful age. Sur. William Miller. Wit. William Price and Pierce Griffin, brother of Nancy. p. 63.

19 November 1799. Robert MILLER and Sarah Johnson. Sur. John Miller. Wit. Andrew Stevenson. p. 63.

15 April 1803. Thomas MILLER and Anne Parker, dau. of Jephta Parker who is surety and makes oath Thomas is over 21. p. 63.

1 December 1792. William MILLER and Elizabeth Kelley, who consents. Sur. and Wit. Ansel George. p. 63.

22 December 1795. Dudley MINER and Anne Goine, of lawful age; dau. of Agness Goine. Sur. Meredith Childers. Wit. Patrick Childress and Wilson Allen. p. 64.

5 June 1795. John MINGE and Sarah Harrison. Sur. Anthony Singleton. p. 64.

16 April 1788. William MINSON and Elizabeth Lawrence. Ishmael and Ann L. Lawrence consent for Elizabeth; no relationship stated. Sur. Charles Irby. Wit. Absalom Lawrence and Absalom Mandly. p. 64.

27 August 1799. William MINSON and Prudence Truman, dau. of Elizabeth Trumand who consents. Sur. John Whitlock. Wit. John Stagg. p. 64.

4 December 1787. Joseph MINTON and Susanna Lewis, dau. of
Thomas Lewis. Sur. John Gordon. Wit. William Cocke and
Jacob Cohen. p. 64.

17 December 1806. Benjamin MITCHELL and Nancy Tyler, dau. of
Mary Tyler who consents. Sur. Pleasant Hazelwood and John
Rogers. Wit. John Tinsley and Fortunatus Green. Nancy is of
lawful age. p. 64.

10 June 1786. Elijah MITCHELL and Nancy Alley, of lawful age;
dau. of Elizabeth Alley. Sur. Benjamin Smoot. Wit. William
Glenn and William Miller. p. 64.

4 June 1785. Hugh MOODY and Frances Fullgham, who consents.
Sur. John Murray. Wit. Francis Edwards. p. 64.

18 July 1806. John MOODY and Anne Swinton. Sur. Andrew Sweeny
who makes oath Anne is over 21. p. 64.

5 November 1807. John MOODY and Martha Ramsbottom. Sur. Richard
Edwards. p. 64.

17 October 1782. Matthew MOODY and Jane Warwick. Sur. William
Rose. p. 64.

26 January 1790. Matthew MOODY and Susanna Pinkney, who consents.
Sur. Anthony Geoghegan. Wit. John Glynn and John Kantzman.
p. 64.

27 March 1795. Philip MOODY and Catharine Moody. Sur. Matthew
Moody. Philip of York County. p. 64.

2 May 1788. Bernard MOORE and Lucy Leiper, niece of And. Leiper
who consents and is surety. Bernard of King William County.
p. 64.

26 February 1790. Jacob MORDECAI and Sarah Baskivell, who consents
Sur. Mason Whitfield. Wit. Robert Murray. p. 65.

4 January 1806. Ganaway MORGAN and Judy Morriss, dau. of Benjamin
Morris who is surety. p. 65.

10 January 1787. Austin MORRIS and Mary Sheppard. Benjamin
Sheppard consents for Mary; no relationship stated. Sur. and
Wit. Philip Sheppard. p. 65.

29 August 1691. James MORRIS and Elizabeth Hollis. Deeds, Wills,
etc., 1688-1697. p. 253.

1695. Robert MORRIS and Ann Redford, widow. Deeds, Wills, etc.,
1688-1697. p. 604.

26 December 1789. Robert MORRIS and Elizabeth Linch, who consents. Sur. William Thorp. Wit. Allen Thorp and Peter Frankling. p. 65.

6 April 1786. Thomas K. MORRIS and Martha Claxton, of lawful age. Sur. Thomas Turpin. Wit. James Trevilian. p. 65.

25 September 1682. John MORTON and widow of John Hues. Deeds, Wills, etc., 1677-1692. p. 225.

12 October 1798. Benjamin MOSBY and Anne Winston. Sur. Hezekiah Mosby. p. 65.

3 June 1794. Hezekiah MOSBY and Elizabeth Winston, who consents. Sur. Isaac Winston, brother of Elizabeth. Wit. Henry Toler, Philip Sheppard, John M. Sheppard. p. 65.

13 December 1796. Joseph MOSBY and Martha Owen, of lawful age; dau. of Judith Owen. Sur. John M. Sheppard. Wit. William Owen. p. 65.

27 May 1794. Samuel MOSBY and Mary Anderson, dau. of Nathaniel Anderson who consents. Sur. William Marshall. Wit. Frs. Tompkins. p. 65.

29 March 1784. William MOSBY and Rebecca Williamson. Susannah Williamson consents for Rebecca; no relationship stated. Sur. Turner Southall. p. 65.

22 November 1708. John MOSEBY and Martha Womack, dau. of Abr. Womack. Deeds & Wills, 1706-1709. p. 188.

Before 5 October 1725. Robert MOSEBY and Agnes Watson, widow of Benjamin Watson. Orphans Court, 1677-1739. p. 53.

Between 1688-1689. Arthur MOSELEY and Sarah Hancock. Deeds, Wills, etc., 1688-1697. p. 97.

17 December 1793. Arthur MOSELEY and Agness Bransford, who consents. Sur. William Russell. Wit. Sarah Russell and John Winfrey. Arthur of Powhatan County. p. 65.

5 January 1793. William Moss and Nancy Anter, dau. of Sarah Anter who consents. Sur. and Wit. Nathaniel Couzins. p. 65.

8 August 1788. Peter MULLIGAN and Kitty Shackleton, who consents. Sur. David Royster. Wit. Thomas Pleasants and Moses Woodfin. p. 65.

22 December 1701. Robert MUMFORD and Martha Kennon, dau. of Col. Richard Kennon. Deeds, Wills, etc., 1697-1704. p. 279. 3T174.

7 June 1782. John MURPHY and Sarah Bryan. John Bryan consents for Sarah; no relationship stated. Sur. Tim Bryan. p. 66.

2 August 1794. Robert MURRAY and Sarah Hardyman, who consents. Sur. Richard P. Courtney. Wit. John Winemore. p. 66.

19 July 1784. Simon MURRAY and Margaret Miller. Sur. John Lynor. p. 66.

23 December 1797. Joseph A. MYERS and Mrs. Elizabeth Ege, widow. Sur. John Dixon. p. 66.

21 August 1793. Lewis MYERS and Anne Smith, dau. of William Smith, deceased. Jesse Blackburn, guardian of Anne, consents for her and is surety. p. 66.

Between 1688-1689. Robert NAPIER and Mary Perrin. Deeds, Wills, etc., 1688-1697. p. 97.

19 November 1783. Travers NASH and Eleanor White. Sur. John White. Travers of Fauquier County. p. 69.

26 January 1789. William NASH and Ann Clark, who consents; dau. of Alice Clark. Sur. William Lipscomb. Wit. Thomas Lipscomb. p. 69.

3 April 1794. Thomas NEAVAL and Lucy Craddock, who consents. Sur. Abraham Lyon. Wit. David Rice, John Sangster, Joseph Dell, Mary Dell. p. 69.

28 January 1784. Alexander NELSON and Anne Matthews, dau. of Samp. Mathews who consents. Sur. John Gunn. Wit. John Coatsworth and John Mathews. p. 69.

17 January 1801. William NETTLES and Polly West, dau. of Whitton West who is surety. p. 69.

23 November 1793. Benjamin NEW and Margaret Kay, who consents. Sur. John New. Wit. William Cook and William ------. Adam Bard makes oath Margaret is over 21. p. 69.

5 February 1790. John NEW and Fanny Blakey, sister of Smith Blakey who states she is of age. Sur. John Roper. Wit. Robert Cradock (?) p. 69.

11 May 1802. John R. NEW and Nancy Frayser, dau. of William Frayser who consents. Sur. George Blakey. Wit. Richard H. Frayser. p. 69.

12 September 1798. Joseph NEW and Mary Jones, of lawful age; dau. of Solomon Jones. Sur. Andrew Williams. p. 69.

26 February 1785. William NEW and Mary White, dau. of Mary White who consents. Sur. George and William Harwood. Wit. William Whitlock. p. 69.

Before 20 September 1695. Richard NEWCOMB and widow of Thomas Charles. Orphans Court, 1677-1739. p. 38.

4 February 1789. William NICE and Rebecca Warrington, who consents. Sur. Jacob Nice. Wit. Henry ----- who certifies Rebecca is over 21. p. 69.

5 August 1794. William NICE and Nancy Cole, who consents. Sur. and Wit. Samuel Coleman. p. 69.

17 April 1786. John NICOLS and Salley Scott. Sur. John ------. p. 69.

10 May 1783. Cornelius NOBLE and Ann Hoye. Sur. Alexander Wylly. p. 69.

5 January 1807. Nathaniel NUCKOLS and Sally Lankaster, dau. of Joseph Lankaster who is surety. p. 70.

Before 5 October 1725. Daniel NUNNALY and Susanna Womack, widow of William Womack. Orphans Court, 1677-1739. p. 54.

3 July 1788. Henry OAKWOOD and Amelia Redding, who consents. Sur. Henry Dinsell. Wit. Amelia Birk and Calvin Sawyer. p. 71.

13 September 1794. Henry P. OATEST and Lucy Lancaster, who consents. Sur. Abraham Dull. Wit. John Lancaster and Margaret Lancaster. p. 71.

7 May 1807. Joseph OLIVER and Ann Elliott, widow. Sur. William Rawleigh. p. 71.

18 January 1787. Vincent OLIVER and Sarah Clark, who consents. Sur. John Courtney. Wit. John and Jane Price. p. 71.

19 July 1787. Robert OMBERSON and Mary Watkins. Sarah Bellimon certifies Mary is her daughter and is over 21. Sur. and Wit. Joseph Harrel. p. 71.

15 June 1694. Edward OSBORNE and Elizabeth Browne. Deeds, Wills, etc., 1688-1697. p. 552.

7 January 1799. Thomas OTEY and Frances Carter. Sur. Moses Woodfin. Wit. Andrew Stevenson. p. 71.

30 December 1698. Samuel OULTON and Sarah Tanner, widow of Joseph Tanner. Deeds, Wills, etc., 1697-1704. p. 144.

3 October 1807. Matthew H. OWEN and Mary Burton, dau. of William Burton who is surety. p. 71.

11 April 1792. John PAGE and Catharine Wassels, who consents.
Sur. James Roberts. Wit. William Adams. p. 73.

4 September 1808. Samuel PAGE and Nancy Smith, both people of
color. Sur. William Ligins. p. 73.

19 November 1807. William B. PAGE and Jane Wiseham. Sur. John
Darmsdatt who makes oath Jane is over 21. p. 73.

2 June 1787. William PALMER and Sary Wood, who consents. Sur.
Joseph Harrel. Wit. John Blakey. p. 73.

17 January 1792. Benjamin PARKER and Nancy Binford, of lawful
age; dau. of Thomas Binford. Sur. James Binford. p. 73.

10 November 1790. John PARKER and Elizabeth Hamblett. Sur.
George Hamblett. p. 73.

17 July 1806. William PARKER and Mary Rountree, ward of Jephta
Parker who is surety. William is son of Jephta. p. 73.

27 September 1786. Woodrow PARSONS and Nancy Mosby, dau. of
John Mosby who consents. Sur. Samuel Mosby. Wit. Jos.
Mosby. p. 73.

10 December 1808. Philip PASLEY and Eliza Booze, who consents.
Sur. Nathaniel Thomson who makes oath Eliza is over 21. p. 73.

27 December 1806. Absalom PATE and Catharine Phillips, dau. of
Mourning Phillips who is surety. p. 73.

5 March 1793. John PATMAN and Elizabeth Smith, dau. of John
Smith who consents. Sur. Watson Patman. Wit. James Branch
and Robert Clark. p. 73.

29 August 1792. Watson PATMAN and Elizabeth Miller, dau. of
William Miller who consents. Sur. John Patman. Wit. Edward
Miller. p. 73.

July 1696. Francis PATRAM and Frances Elam. Deeds, Wills,
etc., 1688-1697. p. 631.

24 January 1783. James PATTERSON and Susannah Matthews, who
consents. Sur. Hutchins Mathews. Wit. Ambrose Jones. p. 73.

1 April 1793. John PATTERSON and Mary Woodward, who consents.
Sur. Samuel Sheppard. Wit. Sam and Charles Woodward. p. 73.

20 December 1794. James PAUL and Ann Dunelwen, widow, who
consents. Sur. and Wit. Francis Muncas and Duke Howers. Ann
of the City of Richmond. p. 73.

17 July 1782. Thomas PAUL and Mary New. Sur. Joseph Castle. p. 74.

10 January 1806. Benjamin PAYNE and Nancy Vaughan. Sur. Joseph Vaughan who makes oath Nancy is over 21. p. 74.

13 October 1797. Joshua PEAKE and Mary Ann Smith. Sur. Thomas Smith. p. 74.

13 September 1802. Francis PEARCE and Elizabeth Redford, dau. of Perrin Redford who is surety. p. 74.

15 February 1790. Joseph PEARCE and Sarah Turpin, who consents. Sur. Michael Turpin. Wit. Tempe Turpin, John Turpin, Jr., Mark Woodcock. p. 74.

16 January 1807. Morgan PEARCE and Lenora Bottom. Sur. George Williamson who is guardian of Morgan and consents for him. p. 74.

22 July 1797. William PEARCE and Patience Redford, dau. of Mary Redford who consents. Sur. William Garthright. Wit. Pearin and Barnet Redford. p. 74.

9 April 1796. James PEARMAN and Lucy Powers. Sur. and Wit. William Pearman. p. 74.

27 October 1787. Janus PEARMAN and Mary Morris, of lawful age. Sur. George Rowland. Wit. George Dickson. p. 74.

29 February 1796. Daniel PECK and Nancy Cocke. Sur. Nathaniel Sheppard. p. 74.

3 December 1802. John PEEK and Rebecca Hogans, dau. of John Hogans who consents and states Rebecca is under 21. Sur. Shepherd Coots. Wit. John Coots. p. 74.

12 November 1807. Robert PEMBERTON and Elizabeth Nagley, dau. of Jacob Nagley. Sur. Joshua Brotherhood who makes oath Elizabeth is over 21. p. 74.

20 December 1784. William PEMBERTON and Marian Binford. Thomas Binford consents for Marian; no relationship stated. Sur. William Hix. Wit. William Binford. p. 74.

5 January 1787. Benjamin PERKINS and Mary Williams, who consents. Sur. and Wit. Peter Sharp. p. 74.

10 June 1799. Nathaniel PERKINS and Lucy Henley, dau. of Leonard Henley who consents. Sur. Turner R. Henley. Wit. John Holman and Hez. Henley. p. 74.

16 January 1790. Anthony PETERS and Druscilla Daily, dau. of Joseph Daily who consents. Sur. Lewis Fortune. Wit. John Livingston. p. 74.

28 April 1807. John PETTUS and Eliza D. Williamson, who consents. Sur. Elisha Price who makes oath Eliza is over 21. p. 74.

14 January 1794. John Frederick PHILLIPE and Sally Clarke, who consents. Sur. Robert Omiston who certifies Sally is over 21. Wit. ----- Gale and ----- Munson. p. 74.

12 December 1807. Isaac PHILLIPS and Elizabeth Grinstead. Sur. James Grinstead who makes oath Elizabeth is over 21. p. 74.

29 May 1807. James PHILLIPS and Jenny, a dark mulatto woman, emancipated by the verdict of the Richmond district. Both registered in Hustings Court. p. 74.

4 November 1806. John PHILLIPS and Mary Philbates, dau. of John Philbates who is surety. Henry Drake makes oath John Phillips is over 21. p. 75.

23 March 1808. Mourning PHILLIPS and Elizabeth Kendrick, dau. of Robert Kendrick who is surety. p. 75.

23 April 1806. Oakley PHILPOTS and Nancy Nash, ward of Humphrey Dabney, of the City of Richmond, who is surety. p. 75.

17 November 1798. Francis PHILPOTTS and Elizabeth Cassey, who consents. Sur. Charles Purcell. Wit. James Newell, Nathaniel Moody, William Mitchell, Chas. Falcom. p. 75.

15 June 1793. Asher PICKET and Mary Peerman, who consents. Sur. John Pearman of Charles City County. Wit. Rebecca Pearman, Samuel Osslin, William -----, Elizabeth -----. p. 75.

16 October 1789. George PICKET and Margaret Flint, who consents. Sur. Andrew Leiper. Wit. M. Gallego. p. 75.

19 April 1793. Francis PICKETT and Sally Wray, of lawful age. Sur. Richard Harwood. Wit. Thomas Clay, Robert Miller, William ------, Kitty Wray. p. 75.

5 March 1697. Francis PIERCE and Katherine Cressy. Deeds, etc., 1697-1699. p. 96.

28 January 1792. Thomas PINCHBACK and Frances Clarke, dau. of B. Clarke who consents. Sur. Robert Throgmorton. Wit. John Throgmorton and John Parker. p. 75.

4 April 1795. Thomas PINCHBACK and Salley Drake, dau. of Benjamin Drake who consents. Sur. James Brown. Wit. Robert Taylor. p. 75.

10 August 1788. Isaac PLANT and Sarah Belemy, widow, who consents. Sur. and Wit. John Miller. p. 75.

15 May 1699. Joseph PLEASANTS and Martha Cocke. Deeds, Wills, etc., 1697-1704. p. 152.

7 November 1792. Joseph PLEASANTS and Frances Price, dau. of Frances Keese who consents. Sur.and Wit. David W. Sharpe and -------- -------. p. 75.

16 May 1807. John Woodson PLEASANTS and Elizabeth W. Coleman, dau. of Samuel Coleman who is surety. p. 75.

18 July 1795. Samuel PLEASANTS and Debby Lownes. Sur. Jesse Thornton. Sally Hewes certifies Debby, daughter of James Lownes, was 21 on 19 February 1795. Wit. Isham B------- and Joseph Lynch. p. 75.

14 March 1806. David POE, Jr. and Eliza Hopkins, widow of Charles D. Hopkins. Sur. James Whitelaw. Eliza of the City of Richmond. p. 75.

28 November 1794. Samuel POINTER and Mary Miller. Sur. David Holloway and Jesse Mims. p. 75.

30 October 1788. Thomas POINTER and Anne French. Samuel Goodman, guardian of Anne, consents and is surety. p. 75.

12 February 1798. William POINTER and Lucy Burns, who consents. Sur. Richard Burns who makes oath Lucy is over 21. Wit. Parke Bailey. Lucy of the City of Richmond. p. 73.

29 November 1786. James POLLARD and Jemima Kent, who consents. Sur. William Shelburn. Wit. Charles Keesee. p. 75.

20 May 1806. William POND and Elizabeth Philbate, dau. of John Philbate who is surety. p. 75.

27 October 1808. Robert POORE and Ann T. Bagners, ward of John B. Walton who is surety. p. 75.

23 April 1784. Nathaniel POPE and Polley DuVal, of lawful age. Sur. Marks Vandevale. Wit. William DuVal. p. 76.

7 July 1787. Pleasant PORTER and Sally Gammon, of lawful age. Sur. and Wit. Charles Webb. p. 76.

22 August 1786. William PORTER and Nancy Alviss. Jesse and Nany Alviss consent for Nancy; no relationship stated. Sur. John Turner. Wit. Benjamin Johnson. p. 76.

6 January 1790. William PORTER and Elizabeth Gardner, who consents. Sur. Patrick Braney who certifies Elizabeth is over 21. Wit. An Braney. p. 76.

26 June 1806. Charles POTTER and Mrs. Ameley Vanderslise. Sur. James Rountree who makes oath Ameley is a resident of the City of Richmond. p. 76.

5 January 1797. John POTTS and Mrs. Anna Evans, who consents. Sur. Gilbert T. Richardson. p. 76.

3 September 1683. Robert POVALL and Elizabeth Hooper. Deeds, Wills, etc., 1677-1692. p. 252.

26 January 1791. Frederick POWELL and Salley Carter, who consents. Sur. Giles Carter. Wit. Jesse Sadler and John Bruce. p. 76.

16 December 1784. William POWELL and Mary Ellis, who consents. Sur. John Liggon. p. 76.

14 June 1790. William POWELL and Elinor Ball, who consents. Sur. Henry Ball who certifies Elinor, his sister, is over 21. Wit. William Smith and Jno. ------. p. 76.

22 December 1797. William POWERS and Anne Peck, widow. Sur. James Carney. p. 76.

11 June 1798. John PRESTON and Mary Radford. William Radford consents for Mary; no relationship stated. Sur. William Temple. Wit. George Prosser and Augustine Davis. p. 76.

12 June 1806. Thomas Lewis PRESTON and Edmonia Madison Randolph, dau. of Edmund Randolph of the City of Richmond. Sur. James Breckenridge. p. 76.

20 August 1691. Henry PREVETT and Rebecca Dobbs. Deeds, Wills, etc., 1688-1697. p. 253.

5 June 1784. David PRICE and Susanna Matthews, who consents. Sur. Jacob Richardson. Wit. Stephen Smithers. p. 76.

14 April 1786. John W. PRICE and Nancy Kennon, who consents. Sur. and Wit. J. E. Price. p. 76.

29 November 1794. Joseph PRICE and Lucy Burton, who consents. Sur. William S. Smith. p. 76.

23 June 1807. Marrin PRICE and Martha Depriest, ward of Braxton Craddock who is surety. p. 76.

27 October 1794. Nathaniel W. PRICE and Jane Chapman. George Green certifies Nicholas Syme, of Hanover County, is the lawful guardian of Jane who is under 21, and a resident of the City of Richmond. Sur. William Temple. Wit. B. Wilson and Elizabeth Green. p. 76.

20 June 1797. Nathaniel W. PRICE and Elizabeth Smith, dau. of
Jesse Smith who consents. Sur. Josephus Fox. Wit. Henry M.
Clatchy. p. 76.

22 November 1786. Peter PRICE and Sarah Hodges. William Ring,
guardian of Sarah, consents for her. Sur. illegible. Wit.
Elisha Price, John W. Price. p. 76.

7 February 1803. Robert PRICE and Susanna Price. Sur. Walter
Shelton. Daniel Price makes oath Robert is over 21. p. 76.

2 July 1793. Samuel PRICE and Elizabeth Price. Sur. Barret
Price. Samuel of Charlotte County. p. 76.

10 February 1795. William PRICE and Lucy DuVal, dau. of William
DuVal who consents. Sur. Robert Carrington. Wit. Andrew
Dunscomb and Mungo Roy, Jr. p. 76.

18 April 1806. Richard PRICHARD and Frances Sharp, widow of
Hales Sharp. Sur. John Parker. p. 77.

24 November 1708. William PRIDE and Anne Hill, widow. Deeds
& Wills, 1706-1709. p. 188.

3 September 1795. David PRIMROSE and Prudence Williamson, who
consents. Sur. Archibald Lang. Wit. Wilson Allen, William
Mann, Thomas A. Taylor. p. 77.

4 January 1789. Noah PRINCE and Anne Ashley, of lawful age.
Sur. Wray Thomas. Wit. Mary Anderson and Rebeker Hale. p. 77.

5 October 1798. John PROSSER and Mary Pool, of lawful age. Sur.
John Butler. Wit. James Brown, John Hargrove, Jr., Susannah
Lewis, Wilson Price. p. 77.

7 December 1796. Edmund PRUELL and Elizabeth Throgmorton, dau.
of Josiah Throgmorton who consents. Sur. John Tupell. Wit.
Joseph Pleasants and Perrin Throgmorton. Benjamin Tupell certifies
Elizabeth is 21. p. 77.

Before 5 October 1725. Womack PUCKET and Mabel Pucket, widow of
William Pucket. Orphans Court, 1677-1739. p. 54.

18 March 1691. John PUCKETT and Elizabeth Allen. Sur. George
Worsham. Deeds, Wills, etc., 1688-1697. p. 357.

13 October 1796. John PUGH and Mrs. Judith Giles. Sur. Andrew
Leiper. Wit. J. Blagrove. p. 77.

19 January 1784. Mosby PULLIAM and Sally Timberlake, who consents.
Sur. Drury Wood. p. 77.

Before 5 October 1725. Page PUNCH and Elizabeth Good, widow of Robert Good. Orpahns Court, 1677-1739. p. 54.

1 February 1790. Jesse PURYEAR and Jane Holman, dau. of Nathaniel Holman who consents. Sur. Thomas Burton. Wit. John Burch and Daniel Burton. p. 77.

7 January 1797. John PURYEAR and Polly Syme, of lawful age. Sur. and Wit. William Cawthon. p. 77.

23 April 1785. Thomas PURYEAR and Jane Johnson. Sur. Ben Johnson. p. 77.

18 April 1794. George PYLE and Elizabeth Cocke, who consents. P. Cocke certifies Elizabeth is his daughter and is lawful age. Sur. Daniel Hooper. Wit. Jeffrey Vandervall. p. 77.

5 July 1798. Valentine QUAREY and Ruth Cawthan, dau. of William Cawthan who is surety. Wit. Robert Mitchell. p. 79.

28 October 1785. Henry QUARLES and Mary Williamson. Sur. John Williamson. p. 79.

---- ---- 1798. Alexander QUARRIER and Sally Burns. Note: Bond torn. p. 79.

23 October 1806. George RABON and Jane Glenn, who consents and states she is of lawful age. Sur. William Glenn. p. 81.

18 August 1796. Andrew RADFORD and Milley Throgmorton. Sur. Pearin Redford. p. 81.

4 February 1792. Edward RADFORD and Polly Cox Radford, dau. of Joseph and Mary Radford who consent. Sur. Joseph Foster. Wit. James Roberts and Pearin Redford. p. 81.

7 August 1794. Robert RADFORD and Ann Price. Sur. James Price. p. 81.

6 April 1807. Richard RAGLAND and Mary H. Parker. Sur. Anderson Crump. p. 81.

16 October 1807. John RAINS and Nancy Carter. Sur. Cyrus Jones who makes oath Nancy is over 21. p. 81.

25 February 1788. Henry RAKES and Elizabeth Warinner, who consents; dau. of Anne Warinner. Sur. James Warinner. Wit. William Jones and George Cash. p. 81.

7 May 1808. Peter RALSTON and Janett Gilchrist, widow. Sur. John Trower. p. 81.

16 January 1783. Isaac RAMSBOTTOM and Katy Mourning. Sur. James Swinton. p. 81.

4 July 1788. Isaac RAMSBOTTOM and Betsey Willis, dau. of William Willis who consents and is surety. p. 81.

7 May 1782. Brett RANDOLPH and Ann Randolph, dau. of Richard Randolph who consents. Sur. St. George Tucker. p. 81.

30 December 1789. Richard RANDOLPH and Judith Randolph, dau. of Thomas M. Randolph who consents. Sur. Archibald Randolph. Wit. H. Randolph. p. 81.

11 September 1790. Thomas M. RANDOLPH and Gabriella Harvie, dau. of John Harvie who consents. Sur. Harry Heath. p. 81.

24 October 1801. William RAWLEIGH and Milley Gibbs, both of the City of Richmond. Sur. Charles Abraham. William Kennedy makes oath Milley is over 21. p. 81.

19 February 1801. Harry REDD and Suky Scott, dau. of William Scott who is surety. Zach. Rowland certifies both Harry and Suky are free born. p. 82.

20 July 1798. Samuel REDD and Polly Scott, widow. Sur. Aaron Smith. p. 82.

20 May 1698. John REDFORD and Martha Milner. Deeds, Wills, etc., 1697-1704. p. 124.

17 October 1798. John REDFORD and Lucy Redford, dau. of Francis Redford who consents. Sur. Josiah Bullington. Wit. William Redford. p. 81.

20 May 1801. Milner REDFORD and Elizabeth Ellis, dau. of John Ellis, deceased. Sur. Thomas Winn, of Goochland County, who makes oath both Milner and Elizabeth are over 21. p. 81.

26 January 1808. Pearin REDFORD and Judith Warriner. Sur. Samuel Warriner who makes oath Judith is over 21. p. 81.

3 April 1800. Richard REDFORD and Sarah Price, dau. of Sarah Price who consents and makes oath Sarah is over 21. Sur. and Wit. John Fleming Price. p. 81.

11 March 1800. Ware REDFORD and Jane Crawford, who consents. Sur. William Pearce who makes oath Jane is daughter of John Crawford, deceased, and is over 21. p. 82.

28 March 1793. William C. REDFORD and Sally Redford, who consents; dau. of Frank Redford. Sur. James Redford. Wit. Ware Redford. p. 82.

30 August 1784. Francis REKOE and Martha Nailer, dau. of Bety
Naler. Sur. and Wit. Joseph Liplong. p. 82.

30 September 1790. William REYNOLDS and Betsey Whitlock, dau.
of Ann Whitlock who consents. Sur. Tarpley White. p. 82.

28 May 1785. Matthew RICHARDSON and Fanny Dailey, dau. of
Joseph Dailey who consents. Sur. William Dailey. p. 82.

6 March 1790. Thomas RIDDLE and Lucy Sneed, dau. of Catharine
Sneed who consents. Sur. Zachariah Bridgwater. Wit. Mary
Sneed. p. 82.

5 November 1794. James RIND and Sarah Seabrook, who consents.
Sur. Bartholomew Trueheart. Wit. John Seabrook, brother of
Sarah. p. 82.

7 February 1807. Thomas RITCHIE and Isabella Foushee, dau. of
W. Foushee who consents. Sur. and Wit. William Foushee, Jr.
p. 82.

24 August 1786. Spencer ROANE and Anna Henry, dau. of P. Henry,
who consents. Sur. Miles Selden. p. 83.

23 December 1786. Charles ROBERTS and Sarah Cammel, who consents.
Sur. Nicholas Peddicoast. Wit. Charles Pearson. p. 83.

17 February 1791. James ROBERTS and Susanna Watkins, dau. of
Sally ----- who consents. Sur. John Lester. Wit. William
Black. Note: Record mutilated. p. 83.

21 January 1792. Joseph ROBERTS and Sarah Williams, dau. of
Jonathan Williams who consents. Sur. Francis Williams. Wit.
John and Elizabeth Williams. p. 83.

6 October 1795. Fields ROBERTSON and Martha Goode, who consents.
Sur. John Robertson. Wit. Thomas Clarke, Martha Clarke, Nancy
Tisdeal. p. 83.

25 April 1808. James ROBERTSON and Charity Clark. Sur. George
Whitlow who makes oath Charity is over 21. p. 83.

21 December 1787. George ROBINSON and Elizabeth W. George of
lawful age; dau. of Elizabeth Lambert. Sur. and Wit. David
Donnan. p. 83.

27 July 1790. George ROBINSON and Mary Tauman, dau. of Abraham
Tauman who consents. Sur. Richard Tauman. Wit. Sherwood
Carter. p. 83.

23 February 1808. Joseph ROBINSON and Martha Enroughty. Sur.
Nathaniel Enroughty. p. 83.

16 April 1808. Peter ROBINSON and Susanna Lindsay, dau. of Moses Lindsay who is surety. p. 83.

3 October 1789. Samuel ROBINSON and Jane Goode, who consents; dau. of Mary Goode. Sur. William Robinson. Wit. Joseph Pleasants and John Robinson. p. 83.

12 June 1795. Charles ROCKE and Mrs. Martha Dorisch. Sur. John Lester. p. 83.

12 September 1799. John ROGERS and Milley Tyler, dau. of Skelton Tyler who is surety. p. 83.

3 December 1781. Shadrick ROGERS and Susanna Warriner. Sur. James Warriner. p. 83.

5 February 1782. William ROLSTON and Martha Kelly. Sur. John Smith. Wit. J. Beckley. p. 83.

24 March 1785. Andrew RONALD and Sarah Payne. Sur. Foster Webb. Wit. William Whitlock. p. 83.

18 May 1807. John ROPER and Maria Gennett. Sur. John Darrom. p. 84.

10 December 1792. Thomas ROSE and Lucy Winston. Sur. John K. Read. p. 84.

5 November 1806. David R. ROSS and Mrs. Elizabeth Webb. Sur. Jacob G. Ege. p. 84.

30 July 1798. James ROUNTREE and Polly Carter, who consents. Sur. Olive Thomas. p. 84.

29 April 1803. John ROUSELL and Dorcas Rogers. Sur. Richard Allen. p. 84.

12 October 1703. William ROWLETT and Frances Worsham. Deeds, Wills, etc., 1697-1704. p. 351.

10 October 1795. John ROYAL and Mary Smith, who consents. Sur. and Wit. Daniel Burton. p. 84.

December 1698. Joseph ROYAL and Elizabeth Kennon. Deeds, Wills, etc., 1697-1704. p. 144.

2 June 1800. David ROYSTER and Elizabeth R. Burton. Sur. and Wit. John Burton. p. 84.

6 May 1784. John ROYSTER and Sarah Farrar, dau. of Joseph R. Farrar who consents. Sur. Robert Watkins. Wit. Rebecah DuVall and William Giles. p. 83.

20 April 1785. Littleberry ROYSTER and Nancy Phariss. Miles Gathright, guardian of Nancy, consents for her and is surety. p. 84.

4 December 1788. William ROYSTER and Elizabeth Turpin, dau. of Luzby Turpin who consents. Sur. William Lipscomb. Wit. John Turpin, Luzby Turpin, Jr., Michael Turpin. p. 84.

2 March 1793. Fleming RUSSELL and Nancy Smith. Sur. John Smith. p. 84.

31 October 1786. William RUSSELL and Sarah Holland, who consents. Sur. Samuel Couch. Wit. Samuel Dyer and James Trigg. Sarah was born in the Parish of St. Albins, City of London. p. 84.

31 December 1787. James RYALL and Lucy Britton, dau. of James Britton. Sur. Edmund Apperson. Wit. John Ryall and Louisea Britton. p. 84.

1 June 1785. Michael RYAN and Frances Dudley. Sur. William Claiborne. p. 84.

27 February 1786. Philip RYLEY and Sarah Bullington, who consents. Sur. and Wit. Thomas Hood. p. 84.

2 January 1787. John SABB and Betsy Berry, who consents. Sur. Matthew Richardson. Wit. William Dailey. p. 85.

6 April 1787. Charles SABLONG and Sally Berry, who consents. Sur. John Tabb. p. 85.

15 October 1785. Jacob SALLEE and Judith Trueman, dau. of Abraham Trueman who consents. Sur. Richard Trueman. p. 85.

22 December 1786. George SALMON and Mary Throgmorton, dau. of Richard Throgmorton who consents and is surety. p. 85.

29 October 1807. John SATTERWHITE and Polly Turpin. Sur. Benjamin DuVal who makes oath Polly is over 21. p. 85.

3 November 1787. Mann SATTERWHITE, Jr. and Nancy Price, dau. of Robert Price who is surety. p. 85.

Before 5 October 1725. John SAUNDERS and Anne Stovall, widow of Bartho. Stovall. Orphans Court, 1677-1739. p. 54.

15 November 1799. George SAVAGE and Elizabeth M. Gathright. Ann Whitlock consents for Elizabeth; no relationship stated. Sur. Samuel Moody. Wit. Southy L. Savage. p. 85.

25 November 1794. William SAVAGE and Salley Whitlock, dau. of Anne Whitlock who consents. Sur. Nathaniel L. Savage. Wit. John Clopton and William Carter. William Savage of New Kent County. p. 85.

18 April 1782. Samuel SCHERER and Hannah Tankard. Sur. John Beckley. p. 85.

4 August 1787. Andrew SCOTT and Milender Scott, dau. of Robert and Mary Scott who consent. Sur. Edward Boman and John Scott. p. 85.

25 February 1792. Francis SCOTT and Rachel Scott, widow. Patience Scott, sister of Rachel, consents for her. Sur. Andrew Scott. p. 85.

3 November 1784. James SCOTT and Rebecca Duval, who consents. Sur. Jos. Duval. Wit. Elizabeth and Benjamin Duval. p. 85.

14 December 1790. James SCOTT and Betsey Clarke. Sur. Thomas Clarke. p. 85.

4 January 1788. John SCOTT and Charity Scott. Consent reads, "We, the parents of John Scott and Charity Scott are agreeable to this marriage". Signed: Robert Scott and Sarah Scott. Sur. Francis Bowman. Wit. Jonathan Williams and Sarah Williams. p. 85.

4 November 1793. John SCOTT and Lucy David, who consents. Sur. Peter Sharpe. Wit. Mich'l. Turpin. p. 85.

23 October 1793. Robert SCOTT and Martha Scott, who consents. Sur. Edward Bowman. p. 86.

Before 15 September 1708. Walter SCOTT and widow of Samuel Branch. Orphans Court, 1677-1708. p. 50.

23 July 1790. Walter SCOTT and Sarah Nichols, who consents. Sur. Peter Hay. Wit. Linas Tait. p. 86.

27 January 1795. John Gordon SCULLY and Elizabeth Smith, of lawful age. Sur. and Wit. Richard Nailor. p. 86.

4 November 1807. Augustine SEATON and Catharine Newman, who consents. Sur. and Wit. William Giles. p. 86.

26 April 1796. George W. SEATON and Polly Howerton. Sur. Thomas Howerton. p. 86.

4 July 1797. John Lewis SESTIE and Clatilda Millet Marchand, who consents. Sur. Lewis M. Rivalain. p. 86.

20 December 1798. William SHACKLETON and Nancy Carter, who consents. Sur. Throdorick Carter. Wit. Frances Carter. William of Chesterfield County. p. 86.

11 October 1793. Michael SHANNON and Phebe Kelley, who consents. Sur. James Bisset. Wit. James Cawthon. p. 86.

29 May 1795. Barvel SHARP and Sally Clarke. Sur. Thomas Clarke. p. 86.

13 May 1793. Isaac SHARP and Anne Turner, who consents. Sur. James Redford. Wit. Elizabeth Sharp and Abraham Childres. p. 86.

5 October 1803. Isaac SHARP and Anna Perry. Sur. William Randolph of Wilton who makes oath Anna is over 21. p. 86.

24 December 1795. Jacob SHARP and Mary Pasley, of lawful age. Sur. and Wit. Philip Pasley, brother of Mary. p. 86.

26 February 1802. David W. SHARPE and Nancy F. Burton, who signs her own consent. Sur. John Burton who makes oath Nancy is over 21. Wit. Frances K. Folkes. p. 86.

3 September 1792. Hales SHARPE and Frances Williams, dau. of Rachel Williams who consents and states Frances is over 21. Sur. Richard Sharp. Wit. John ------ and Roland Bottoms. p. 86.

17 December 1788. Peter SHARPE and Nancy Price, dau. of Frances Price who consents. Sur. and Wit. Andrew Frayser and William Cocke. p. 86.

26 January 1807. Thomas SHAW and Judith Smoote, dau. of Benjamin Smoote who consents. Sur. and Wit. Barton Smoote. p. 86.

7 January 1784. John SHELTON and Anne Southall. Sur. William DuVal. John of Hanover County. p. 86.

21 March 1807. John SHELTON and Sarah Boyce. Sur. Jos. Boyce. p. 86.

15 January 1800. Walter SHELTON and Anne Price. Sur. John Price. p. 86.

17 June 1799. Pressly SHEPHARD and Sally Phillips, dau. of Larkin Phillips who consents. Sur. and Wit. Joseph Hooker. p. 86.

16 June 1800. Frank SHEPPARD and Jamima Lewis, dau. of Frank Lewis who is surety. R. Gamble testifies to the best of his knowledge Frank is a free born man. p. 87.

16 December 1789. John M. SHEPPARD and Sarah Pulliam. Sur. Thomas Prosser. p. 87.

21 December 1792. Joseph SHEPPARD and Judith Brown, dau. of J. Brown who consents. Sur. George Laughlin. p. 87.

19 April 1794. Nathaniel SHEPPARD and Nancy Pointer, who consents. Sur. Baltaser Dorisch. Wit. Eliza Quarrer, Thomas Pointer, Samuel Pointer. p. 87.

24 April 1793. Reubin SHEPPARD and Salley Cocke, dau. of Richard Cocke who consents. Sur. Joseph DuVal. p. 87.

3 December 1787. Samuel SHEPPARD and Polly Allen, of lawful age; dau. of David Allen, deceased, and Mary Allen. Sur. John Price. p. 87.

9 July 1796. William SHEPPARD and Fanny Shaw, dau. of Elizabeth Shaw who consents. Sur. Peter Cottrell. p. 87.

7 September 1801. Francis SHEPPERSON and Elizabeth Cornet. Sur. Thomas Burton. Allen Cornet makes oath Elizabeth is over 21. p. 87.

9 November 1797. William SHEPPERSON and Anne Blackburn, dau. of William Blackburn who consents. Sur. Nathaniel Blackburn. Wit. Absalem Blackburn. p. 87.

4 September 1806. Holman SHOEMAKER and Elizabeth Ford, dau. of John Ford who consents. Holman is son of Thomas Shoemaker who is surety. p. 87.

19 May 1786. Jeremiah SHOEMAKER and Priscilla Jones, dau. of Priscilla Jones who consents. Sur. Jacob Ellis. Wit. George and Frederick Jude. p. 87.

22 January 1795. Henry SHORE and Patsy Winston. Mary Winston certifies Martha Bickerton Winston is 21 years of age. Sur. John D. Blair. Wit. Eliza Taylor and William Radford. p. 87.

6 February 1806. William SHORT and Jemima Jones, of the City of Richmond. Sur. Samuel Jones who makes oath Jemima is over 21. p. 87.

26 March 1799. Alexander SIMMS and Elizabeth Jordan, dau. of Noble Jordan who is surety. p. 87.

8 October 1788. Anthony SINGLETON and Lucy Randolph, who consents. Sur. John Groves. Wit. John Scruggs, W. Philex, John Hopewell, Thos. Speers. p. 88.

16 July 1699. Edward SKERME and Priscilla Branch. Deeds, Wills, etc., 1697-1704. p. 152.

14 April 1797. Abraham SKIPWITH and Chloe Jones. Sur. and Wit. John Hope. p. 88.

19 December 1794. William SLAYBURN and Elizabeth Miller, who consents; dau. of Thomas Miller. Sur. and Wit. Joseph Harrel. p. 88.

10 November 1807. Pleasant SMETHE and Polley P. Carter, who consents. Sur. Moses Carter who makes oath Polly is over 21. Wit. Polley Austin. p. 88.

6 February 1793. George W. SMITH and Sally Adams. Sur. William Marshall. p. 88.

21 October 1800. Hampshire SMITH and Rachel Meadows, who consents. Sur. Toby Jackson. p. 88.

26 October 1797. Jacob SMITH and Martha Lennard, of lawful age. Martha is daughter of John Lennard, deceased. Sur. and Wit. Elisha Price. p. 88.

20 February 1806. Jacob SMITH and Tabitha Burton, dau. of John Burton who is surety. p. 88.

29 March 1805. Jesse SMITH and Lucy Cocke, widow of Robert Cocke. Sur. Elisha Price. p. 88.

10 August 1787. Johnson SMITH and Anne Scott, of lawful age. Anne is daughter of Nanny Scott. Sur. Axam Scott. p. 88.

24 December 1794. Landon SMITH and Lucy Ruffin, who consents; dau. of Molly Norman. Sur. Jesse Scott. Wit. James Wray, John Lester, James Redford. p. 88.

1695. Robert SMITH and Sus. Holmes, Deeds, Wills, etc., 1688-1697. p. 604.

19 February 1787. Samuel SMITH and Tabitha B. Laughlin, dau. of Thomas Laughlin, Sr. who consents and is surety. p. 88.

28 June 1788. Samuel SMITH and Nancy Carserean, who consents. Sur. James Bisset. Wit. John Sangster and William Corling. p. 88.

2 December 1797. Thomas SMITH and Sarah Linnard, ward of John Price, who consents. Sur. and Wit. Jacob Smith. Sarah daughter of John Linnard, deceased. p. 88.

15 August 1787. William SMITH and Elizabeth White, of lawful age. Elizabeth is daughter of David White, deceased. Sur. and Wit. John White. p. 89.

1 January 1789. William SMITH and Elizabeth Crouch, dau. of
Richard Crouch who consents. Sur. Richard Crouch, Jr. Wit.
Nathaniel Anderson and William Bailey. p. 89.

13 October 1797. William SMITH and Elizabeth Howerton, of
lawful age. Sur. James Howerton, brother of Elizabeth. p. 89.

5 March 1799. William SMITH and Lucy Emmory. Sur. John
Williamson and Thomas Pinchback. p. 89.

31 December 1802. William SMITH and Sarah Perry. Sur. James
Hill. p. 89.

26 February 1798. Barton SMOOT and Mary Alley. Sur. William
Alley. p. 89.

4 August 1806. Josiah SMOOT and Elizabeth Brown, dau. of Micajah
Brown who consents. Sur. Barton Smoot. Wit. William and Daniel
Brown. p. 89.

13 February 1796. Herman B. C. SNEED and Sophia Williamson, dau.
of George Williamson who is surety. p. 89.

28 March 1788. John SNEED and Patsy Walton, dau. of John Walton
who consents. Sur. John L. Walton. Wit. Benjamin Walton.
p. 89.

9 February 1795. Patrick SNEED and Elizabeth Gathright, who
consents. Sur. Nathaniel Holman. Wit. John Holman and O.
Gathright. p. 89.

16 April 1802. William SNEED and Sally Phillips, dau. of Larkin
Phillips who is surety. p. 89.

14 November 1791. John SOUTHWARD and Bittey Muse, who consents.
Sur. Theodorick Massie. Wit. Jeremiah Burton and Thomas Southworth. p. 89.

17 April 1792. Thomas SOUTHWORTH and Mrs. Mary Williamson who
consents. Sur. and Wit. Theodorick Massie. p. 89.

25 September 1794. Robert Taylor SPARKS and Elizabeth Parker.
Sur. Jepthey Parker. p. 89.

3 May 1783. John SPEARS and Patsey Harwood, dau. of Bathsheba
Harwood who consents. Sur. George Harwood. p. 89.

13 September 1783. Robert SPEARS and Agness Gathright. Sur.
George Harwood. p. 89.

26 December 1801. Robert SPENCE and Sarah Lacey, widow of William
Lacey. Sur. John McLeod and James Davenport. p. 89.

14 September 1795. Charles SPENCER and Elizabeth Wray Carter, dau. of William Carter, Sr. who consents. Sur. William Hawkins. p. 89.

9 April 1807. Joseph SPICER and Polly Beveridge, dau. of Moses Beveridge, deceased. Sur. Perry Clark who makes oath Polly is over 21. p. 89.

19 December 1807. Elias SPRAGUE and Coley Franklin. Sur. William Doyle. p. 89.

19 February 1791. William SPUR and Polley Thomas, dau. of Polley Thomas who consents. Sur. John Meanley. Wit. David Perkins. p. 89.

17 April 1782. John SPURLOCK and Charlotte Mills. Sur. Erasmus Rountree. p. 89.

3 September 1683. Will STACY and Mary Lynn. Deeds, Wills, etc., 1677-1692. p. 252.

Before 5 October 1725. Edward STANLEY and Martha Blankenship, widow of Ralph Blankenship. Orphans Court, 1677-1739. p. 53.

26 November 1806. Edward C. STANNARD and Rebecca Carter. George Hay, guardian of Rebecca, consents for her. Sur. Alex. McRae. Wit. E. Rawlins and Ben Mosby. p. 90.

3 June 1786. James STANTON and Judith Childress, dau. of Robert Childress who consents. Sur. Abraham Spencer. Wit. Cornelias Scully. p. 90.

11 October 1806. Thomas STANTON and Grisilda Leiscester. Sur. Alexander Quarrier. Grisilda of the City of Richmond. p. 90.

19 November 1787. Nathaniel STAPLES and Judith Clarke. William Garthright, guardian of Judith, consents for her. Sur. and Wit. William Clark. p. 90.

15 August 1796. Samuel STAPLES and Betsey Jones, of lawful age. Sur. John Eubank, Jr. Wit. Nathaniel Staples. p. 90.

25 April 1808. William STAPLES and Susanna Griffin, dau. of Pierce Griffin who is surety. p. 90.

26 September 1799. Wilson STAPLES and Patsy Jones, dau. of Langston Jones who is surety. Wit. Nathaniel Staples. p. 90.

18 August 1801. Wilson STAPLES and Susanna Gennett. Sur. James Camp. James Holloway makes oath Susanna is over 21. p. 90.

7 January 1784. Bowling STARKE and Mrs. Anna Orr. Sur. John Pendleton. p. 90.

10 March 1802. William STARKE and Betsey Jones. Sur. Robert Thomson who makes oath Betsey is over 21. p. 90.

3 February 1791. William STARR and Nancy Pearson, dau. of Sarah Pearson who consents. Sur. Robert McKim. Wit. William McKim. p. 90.

3 March 1802. Samuel STEPHEN and Biddy, both free colored people emancipated by Robert and Samuel Pleasants. Sur. and Wit. Peter Sharp. p. 90.

December 1698. Daniel STEWARD and Elizabeth Harloe. Deeds, Wills, etc., 1697-1704. p. 144.

Between 1685-1686. John STEWARD and Susannah Burton. Deeds, Wills, etc., 1677-1692. p. 389.

24 February 1784. John STEWART and Catharine Hare. Zach. Rowland, guardian of Catharine, consents for her and is surety. p. 90.

1 July 1784. William STEWART and Kesiah Dailey, dau. of Lee ------ who consents. Sur. George Muter. p. 90.

8 August 1693. Bar. STOVALL and Ann Burton. Sur. Jno. Steward. Deeds, Wills, etc., 1688-1697. p. 435.

29 December 1786. Littleberry STOVALL and Elizabeth Prosser, who consents. Sur. John Strobia. Wit. Molley Strobia. p. 90.

21 August 1794. Duke STOWERS and Jenny Davis, who consents. Sur. James Bisset. Wit. Isaac Ramsbottom. p. 90.

22 October 1789. Benjamin STRANGE and Molley Bottom. Thomas Bottom consents; no relationship stated. Sur. Peter Leneve. Wit. Pleasant Bottom and Francis Bottom. p. 90.

16 December 1807. James STRATTON and Ann Collins. Sur. William McCabe who makes oath Ann is over 21. p. 90.

24 October 1794. John STREET and Nancy Duvall, who consents. Sur. Joseph Duvall. Wit. Benjamin Duvall. John of Powhatan County. p. 90.

6 May 1788. William STRICKER and Judah Harding, who consents. Sur. Jesse Harding. Wit. William Murray. p. 91.

19 December 1786. Joel STURDIVANT and Frances W. Burnett, who consents. Sur. Nathaniel Dunn. Wit. J. Parker and Sarah Younghusband. p. 91.

8 April 1801. John SUITER and Precilla Brown, widow. Sur. Joseph Selden. p. 91.

6 November 1786. John SULLIVAN and Rhoda Flemmon, widow, who consents. Sur. John Emmons. Wit. William Irby. p. 91.

30 December 1793. Laurence SULLY and Sally Annis, dau. of Sarah Russell who consents. Sur. John Wilson. p. 91.

2 April 1799. Matthew SULLY and Martha Miller, widow of Richard Miller. Sur. William H. Fitzwhylson. p. 91.

25 August 1792. Sam SWANN and Eliza Galt, who consents. Sur. and Wit. David Lambert. p. 91.

12 July 1798. James SWINTON, Jr. and Mary Charles, who consents. Sur. Andrew Caslten. James son of James Swinton, Sr. p. 91.

10 June 1795. John C. SYBOL and Mrs. Peggy Drummond. Sur. Charles Perley. p. 91.

7 April 1796. Robert SYDNOR and Sally Weymouth, of lawful age. Sur. and Wit. John F. Price. p. 91.

7 December 1801. Robert SYDNOR and Lucy Taylor. Sur. James Ratcliffe who makes oath Lucy is over 21. p. 91.

18 December 1800. William TALLEY and Franky Woody. Sur. Henry Cary who makes oath Franky is over 21. p. 93.

19 January 1793. Austin TALMAN and Martha Turpin, who consents. Sur. William Wilkinson. Wit. John Turpin and Lucy Bullington. p. 93.

7 February 1807. Austin TALMAN and Elizabeth Frayser, who consents William Frayser, father of Elizabeth, certifies she is over 21. Sur. Edward Wanton. Wit. Saley Frayser and Beverly Turpin. p. 93.

By December 1682. Joseph TANNER and Ann Floyd. Deeds & Wills, 1677-1692. p. 228.

Between October 1688-1689. Joseph TANNER and Sarah Turpin. Deeds, Wills, etc., 1688-1697. p. 97.

21 July 1794. Benjamin TATE and Anne Poe. Sur. Thomas Poe. p. 93.

12 August 1807. Beverley C. TAYLOR and Elizabeth Ann Hudson. Sur. Joseph Y. Hudson. p. 93.

6 February 1790. James TAYLOR and Dolly Miller, dau. of John Miller who consents. Sur. Richard Kimbrough. Wit. Anthony Sydnor. p. 93.

15 May 1792. John TAYLOR and Sarah Green. Sur. James Green.
Wit. C. Worthy Stephenson. p. 93.

28 August 1807. Joseph TAYLOR and Elizabeth Keesee, dau. of
Charles Keesee who consents. Sur. William Taylor. Wit. Lucy
Berry. p. 93.

Before 5 October 1725. Michael TAYLOR and Dorcas Vaulton, widow
of John James Vaulton. Orphans Court, 1677-1739. p. 54.

13 December 1782. Miles TAYLOR and Martha Edwards. Sur. John
Taylor. p. 93.

10 May 1806. Richardson TAYLOR and Lucy Carter, ward of William
Dawson, of the City of Richmond, who is surety. p. 93.

29 July 1786. Robert TAYLOR and Rebecca Ball, who consents.
Sur. Lewis Ball. Wit. James Figg, Matthew Pate, Thomas Ball,
James Taylor. p. 93.

11 April 1807. Thomas TAYLOR and Lucy Singleton. Sur. William
Marshall. p. 93.

1 September 1784. Joseph TENSHION and Susannah Hogg, who consents.
Sur. James Valentine. Wit. I. Cole. p. 93.

20 November 1797. Randol THACKER and Agathy Bailess, of lawful
age. Sur. James Wood. Wit. Thomas and Mary Bailess. p. 94.

29 September 1791. Allen THARP and Tabitha Nance. Sur. James
Nance. p. 94.

8 April 1782. Jacob THOMAS and Anne Patman. Sur. William Patman.
p. 94.

16 April 1791. William THOMAS and Milley James, who consents.
Sur. Cab'l. Pleasants. Wit. Margaret Pleasants and Ann Thomas
Thompson. p. 94.

27 February 1789. John THOMASON and Alley Morris. James
Richardson, guardian of Alley, consents for her and is surety.
p. 94.

12 February 1806. James THOMPSON and Sally Gadberry, dau. of
John Gadberry who consents. Sur. Nathaniel Holman. Wit.
B----- Williams, Philip Jennings, Thomas Drake. p. 94.

20 December 1806. John THOMPSON and Nancy Chappell. Sur. Foster
Higgins who makes oath Nancy is over 21. p. 94.

2 May 1792. Robert THOMPSON and Sarah Muncas, who consents. Sur.
James Duke. Wit. Frances Muncas. p. 94.

1 May 1784. Thomas THOMPSON and Nancey Pleasants. Sur. Isaac Younghusband. p. 94.

21 February 1806. Thomas J. THOMPSON and Sarah Hundley. Sur. Thomas Gould who makes oath Sarah is over 21 and a resident of the City of Richmond. p. 94.

1 April 1800. William THOMPSON and Lucy Tate, widow. Sur. William Waddy of Louisa County. p. 94.

5 February 1806. William M. THOMPSON and Frances Willis, ward of John Davenport, of the City of Richmond, who is surety. p. 94.

14 October 1783. John THORNBURN and Judith Miller. Sur. John Martin. p. 94.

1 June 1792. Francis THORNTON and Sally Innis. Sur. James Innes. p. 94.

30 August 1808. Pleasant THORP and Nancy Allen, dau. of James Allen who is surety. p. 94.

24 December 1794. James THROGMORTON and Elizabeth Enrufty, of lawful age. Sur. and Wit. Edward Dailey, uncle of Elizabeth. p. 94.

28 January 1802. Jesse THROGMORTON and Polly Sharp, dau. of Hales Sharp, deceased. Sur. Benjamin Goode. p. 94.

14 July 1796. Josiah THROGMORTON and Mary Childers, of lawful age. Sur. and Wit. James Childers. p. 94.

28 January 1797. Josiah THROGMORTON and Sarah Roberts, widow. Sur. Francis Williams. p. 94.

7 March 1801. Robert THROGMORTON and Sarah Robinson. Sur. James Wray who makes oath Sarah is over 21. p. 94.

4 October 1803. Samuel THROGMORTON and Lucy Williams. Sur. Andrew Radford. p. 95.

16 August 1792. Andrew THURMAN and Makey Hogg, who consents. Sur. Richard Allen. p. 95.

24 November 1701. James THWEATE and Judith Soane. Deeds, Wills, etc., 1697-1704. p. 279.

22 September 1808. Curtis TIGNOR and Susanna Freeman, who consents Sur. Charles Barker who makes oath Susanna is over 21. p. 95.

18 November 1794. Daniel TIMMINGS and Elizabeth Raley, who consents. Sur. James Boulton. Wit. Sarah Boulton. p. 95.

4 January 1793. John TINSLEY and Elizabeth Sharpe, dau. of James Sharp, who consents. Sur. William Allen. Wit. J. Tucker and Thomas B. Adams. p. 95.

29 November 1797. John TINSLEY and Patsey Cauley Brown. Sur. Micajah Brown. p. 95.

9 June 1807. John TINSLEY and Precilla Mauzey. Sur. Thomas Clarke. Robert Kennedy makes oath Precilla is over 21. p. 95.

22 October 1804. William TINSLEY and Sarah Mitchell Eubank, dau. of John Eubank who is surety. p. 95.

10 February 1806. James TIPPET and Nancy Blakey. Sur. Arch. Meanley. p. 95.

18 January 1806. James TODD and Susanna Loving, dau. of Richard Loving who is surety. George Todd states his son, James Todd, was born 5 December 1784. Wit. Robert Todd and Thos. Darby. p. 95.

3 March 1807. Samuel TODD and Charity Dabney. Sur. Edward Hallam. p. 95.

15 January 1800. William TODD and Elizabeth Gary, widow. Sur. Jacob Thomas. William of the City of Richmond. p. 95.

29 November 1793. Samuel TOLER and Sally Winston. Thomas Prosser, guardian of Sally, consents for her. Sur. Henry Toler. Wit. David Toler. p. 95.

17 September 1796. David TOMES and Elizabeth Porter, of lawful age. Sur. and Wit. Robert Fraser. p. 95.

28 March 1796. John TOMS and Rebecca Wade, of lawful age. Sur. and Wit. Landy Wade. p. 95.

8 November 1792. John TOWNES and Elizabeth Lewis. Sur. G. Laughlin. p. 95.

5 December 1695. Will TRAYLOR and Judith Archer. Sur. Peter Jones. Deeds, Wills, etc., 1688-1697. p. 631.

Before 1 October 1695. Henry TRENT and Elizabeth Sherman, dau. of Henry Sherman. Deeds & Wills, 1688-1697. p. 595.

October 1688. Samuel TROTTMAN and Mrs. Lewis, widow. Deeds, Wills, etc., 1688-1697. p. 20.

20 February 1797. John TROWER and Mary Wise, of lawful age. Sur. and Wit. Ninnan Wyse. p. 96.

5 November 1790. Bartholomew TRUEHEART and Mary Seabrook. Note: Bond faded name of surety not legible. p. 96.

14 February 1807. Mark TRUEMAN and Rebecca Bethell, dau. of William Bethell who consents. Sur. Reuben West. Wit. John West and Rebecah Bethell. p. 96.

6 October 1806. Daniel TUCKER and Elizabeth Jones, dau. of Jane Jones who makes oath Elizabeth is over 22 years of age. Sur. Richard Allen. p. 96.

4 February 1806. Gideon TUCKER and Catharine S. Ellison. Sur. Daniel Tyler who makes oath Catharine is over 21. p. 96.

19 December 1793. John TUCKER and Barbery Franklin, who consents. Barbery is widow of Peter Franklin. Sur. James Mantelon. Wit. John Emery. p. 96.

5 June 1794. Stookes TUNSTALL and Martha Purket, who consents. Sur. Isaac Pears. Wit. Agness Pears. p. 96.

9 September 1802. Ambrose TURNER and Mary Browning. Sur. John Browning who makes oath both Ambrose and Mary are over 21. p. 96.

12 December 1789. Arthur TURNER and Jenny Crain, dau. of Lilly Crain who consents. Sur. Thomas Jennings. p. 96.

28 December 1797. David TURNER and Martha Wicker, dau. of William Wicker who is surety. p. 96.

10 March 1797. John TURNER and Sally Gathright. Sur. Benjamin Heningham. p. 96.

23 November 1801. John TURNER and Sarah Pickett. Sur. Peter Tender who makes oath Sarah is a widow and a resident of the City of Richmond. p. 96.

13 February 1796. Matthew TURNER and Polly Farmer, who consents. Sur. John Williams. Wit. James Franklin. p. 96.

11 January 1791. Samuel TURNER and Susanna Franklin, who consents. Sur. George Melton. Wit. John Lucas, Nancy Lucas, Samuel Turner, Samuel Ford, Cuthbert Ford. p. 96.

17 July 1788. William TURNER and Nancy Bowers, of lawful age. Nancy is daughter of Pernepy Bowers. Sur. Hezekiah Ford. Wit. Lankston Ford. p. 96.

10 February 1791. Alexander TURPIN and Elizabeth Woodcock, who consents. Sur. and Wit. Henry Woodcock. p. 96.

9 May 1806. John TURPIN and Harriet Gunn. John Gunn consents for Harriet; no relationship stated. Sur. George Scherer. Wit. John Gunn, Jr. p. 96.

9 March 1808. John TURPIN and Sarah Finny. William Mann, guardian of Sarah, consents for her. Sur. John Mann. Wit. Henry Rees. p. 96.

8 May 1786. Luzby TURPIN and Martha Bullington, who consents. Sur. James Redford. Wit. Michael Turpin and Moses A. Myers. p. 97.

4 February 1801. Miles TURPIN and Fanny Frayser, dau. of Jackson Frayser who is surety. p. 97.

11 January 1793. Daniel TYLER and Ann Rita Ellyson. Sur. Elisha Talley. p. 97.

13 February 1782. John TYLER and Sarah Valentine. Sur. James Valentine. p. 97.

1 December 1795. Jones TYLER and Lucy Forde, dau. of Sherwood Forde who is surety. p. 97.

28 January 1796. Pleasant TYLER and Anne Valentine. Sur. James Valentine. p. 97.

8 April 1788. Samuel TYLER and Susanna Jones, of lawful age. Sur. and Wit. Absolum Jones, brother of Susanna. p. 97.

28 August 1792. William TYLER and Rachel Burton, of lawful age. Sur. and Wit. Richard Allen. p. 97.

6 April 1807. William TYLER and Kuzzy Kersey. Sur. Allen Tyler. William is guardian of Kuzzy. p. 97.

1 August 1807. William TYLER and Elizabeth Heath, dau. of Thomas Heath who consents. Sur. Thomas Williams. Wit. Tommy Tugmotton. p. 97.

2 December 1791. Thomas TYREE and Nancy Lowary, who consents. Sur. Stephen Mallory. Wit. John Browning and Absolum Jinkins. p. 97.

22 December 1792. Ralph UMPHRIES and Agness Elerson. Sarah Elerson consents for Agness; no relationship stated. Sur. John White. Wit. Elisha Talley. p. 99.

4 June 1787. James URQUHART and Pinelope Malony. Sur. John Conner p. 99.

5 May 1787. John URQUHART and Catharine King, widow, of lawful age. Sur. James Urquhart and James Drummond. p. 99.

16 November 1787. John URQUHART and Lucy Lepettit. Sur. James Urquhart and William Russell. p. 99.

2 January 1796. James VALENTINE and Mary Hazlewood, of lawful age. Sur. John Tyler. Wit. Sarah Hazlewood. p. 101.

28 December 1791. Zackariah VALENTINE and Patsey Franklin. Sur. Thomas Franklin. p. 101.

16 October 1789. Markes VANDERVALL and Susanna M. Lewis, who consents. Sur. John Gunn. p. 101.

26 May 1807. Nelson P. VANDERVALL and Nancy L. M. Jones. Sur. John Jackson. p. 101.

27 July 1793. Francis VANET and Rosetta Bromfield, who consents. Sur. James Wray. Wit. German Belhoste. p. 101.

29 January 1787. John VAUGHAN and Elizabeth Goyne, who consents. Elizabeth is daughter of Aggy Goyne. Sur. John Goyne. Wit. Anne Goyne. p. 101.

27 August 1806. John VAUGHAN and Nancy Powers. Sur. John Brown who makes oath both John and Nancy are over 21. p. 101.

24 December 1799. Joseph VAUGHAN and Rebecca Blackburn, dau. of John Blackburn. Joseph is son of Littleberry Vaughan. Sur. John Brown who makes oath both Joseph and Rebecca are over 21. p. 101.

29 September 1806. Robert VAUGHAN and Polly Adams Fussell. Sur. Benjamin Fussell. p. 101.

10 January 1798. Samuel VAUGHAN and Betsy Smoot, dau. of Benjamin Smoot who is surety. p. 101.

20 August 1800. William VAUGHAN and Frances Sheppard, widow. Sur. John Broun who makes oath William is over 21. p. 101.

2 February 1792. Richard C. C. VAUGHN and Anne Whitlow, who consents. Sur. Jephty Parker. Wit. Thomas Pinchback and John Parker. p. 101.

Before 15 September 1708. John James VAULTON and Dorcas Lester, widow of John Lester. Orphans Court, 1677-1739. p. 51.

25 June 1807. Joseph VIGLINS and Mary Beale, dau. of John Beale who is surety. p. 101.

13 November 1787. James WADDILL and Ann Biggen, of lawful age. Sur. and Wit. William Patman. p. 103.

2 December 1786. William WADDILL and Nancy Aven. Samuel Dobie, guardian of Nancy, consents for her. Sur. John McEnery. Wit. John Hart and Edmund McNair. p. 103.

21 August 1789. Edward WADE and Elizabeth Thurman, who consents. Sur. Richard Allen. Wit. Libbleberry Allen. p. 103.

2 August 1797. Joseph WADE and Elizabeth Ellis, widow, who consents. Sur. James Mantelow. p. 103.

22 January 1790. Landy WADE and Sarah Echoe, dau. of Isaac Echoe who consents and is surety. Wit. William Pemberton. p. 103.

23 February 1808. Littleberry WADE and Elizabeth Whitis. Sur. John Whitis. p. 103.

11 February 1795. Pleasant WADE and Darkis Hamblett. Sur. George Hamblett who certifies Darkis is over 21. p. 103.

2 April 1791. Robert WADE and Susanna Hill. Sur. Gideon Hill. p. 103.

18 May 1807. Wyatt WADE and Kesiah Bethell. Sur. Elisha Bethell who makes oath Kesiah is over 21. p. 103.

4 April 1803. Samuel WALKER and Elizabeth Holman, dau. of Nath'l. Holman, Sr. who is surety. Samuel is son of Shadrack Walker who consents for him. Wit. Henry and Betsey Holman. p. 103.

21 February 1789. Thomas WALKER and Beckie Walton Pearson, dau. of Sarah Pearson who consents. Sur. Jesse Bowles. Wit. Chisholm Austin. p. 103.

30 January 1793. George WALTON and Nancy Sharp, who consents. Sur. John L. Walton. Wit. John Harwood and Isaac Sharp. p. 103.

Before 5 October 1725. James WALTON and Margaret Dupray, widow of Thomas Dupray. Orphans Court, 1677-1739. p. 54.

14 December 1796. John WALTON, Sr. and Sally Piles, who consents. Sur. Benjamin Walton. Wit. Thomas Orring. p. 104.

3 December 1800. Edward WANTON and Elizabeth Talman Turpin. Sur. Austin Talman who makes oath Elizabeth is over 21. p. 104.

September 1696. Richard WARD and Elizabeth Blackman. Sur. Thomas Cocke, Sr. Deeds, Wills, etc., 1688-1697. p. 631.

31 December 1782. William WARD and Sarah Burton. Sur. John Burton. William of Prince Edward County. p. 104.

March 1708. Caleb WARE and Bethenia Douglas, widow. Deeds & Wills, 1706-1709. p. 188.

19 February 1782. John WARNER and Martha Warner. Sur. Trusman Warner. p. 104.

31 December 1799. Samuel WARRENER and Mary Bethell, dau. of William Bethell who is surety. p. 104.

12 December 1787. Mordecai WARRINER and Betsey Kinsey Pankey, dau. of Samuel Pankey who consents. Sur. John Warriner. Wit. Thomas Pankey. p. 104.

1 November 1784. Trueman WARRINER and Jane Fussell, ward of Samuel Garthright, Sr. who consents. Sur. John Whitlock. p. 104.

29 December 1806. David WATKINS and Nancy Garthright, dau. of Ephriam Garthright who consents. Sur. Tarpley Garthright. Wit. Moses Woodfin, Susanna Woodfin, James Binford. David of Powhatan County. p. 104.

29 September 1807. Peter WATKINS and Dolly, a free black woman. Sur. Stephen Phillips. p. 104.

22 October 1783. Thomas WATKINS and Rebecca Selden. Sur. Bernard Webb. Thomas of Chesterfield County. p. 104.

24 March 1802. Richard WATSON and Susan Price, dau. of James Price who consents. Sur. Edward C. Davis. Wit. Sally Price, Mary B. Sydnor, Eli Price. p. 104.

18 December 1797. George WATT and Margaret Dunn. Sur. William Dunn. p. 104.

22 August 1801. Edmund WAYMOUTH and Frances Davenport. Sur. Pleasant Hazlewood who makes oath Frances is over 21. p. 104.

5 January 1790. John WAYMOUTH and Nancy Davenport, dau. of Martin Davenport who consents and is surety. p. 104.

5 August 1790. William Walker WAYMOUTH and Elizabeth Hudson, dau. of Turner H. Hudson who consents. Sur. John Lester. Wit. Thomas Block and Joseph Elam. p. 104.

19 November 1783. William WEATHERLEY and Nancy Morsing. Sur. James Swinton. p. 104.

21 September 1785. Foster WEBB and Theodocia Cock. Jesse Roper consents for Theodocia; no relationship stated. Sur. George Webb, Jr. p. 104.

By 20 September 1695. Giles WEBB and widow of Henry Randolph. Orphans Court, 1677-1739. p. 38.

5 October 1793. John WEBBER and Keturah Holman, dau. of Nathaniel Holman who consents. John, son of William Webber of Goochland County who consents for him. Sur. Hezekiah Puryear. Wit. Mary Webber, Philip Johnson, Mary Holman Bowles, Henry Holman. p. 104.

1 April 1795. Elisha WEEKS and Sally Ford. Sur. Samuel Ford. p. 105.

22 May 1806. Louis WERCY and Victoire Celeste Cany, dau. of Louis Cany, of the City of Richmond, who is surety. p. 105.

15 May 1794. Claiborne WEST and Martha Clarke, of lawful age; dau. of Anne Clarke. Sur. and Wit. Nathaniel Enroughty. p. 105.

12 July 1790. Edward WEST and Elizabeth Povall, widow, who consents. Sur. James Richardson. Wit. James Pollard, Peter West, Jemima Pollard, William Smith, John Barker. p. 105.

29 June 1808. John L. WEST and Mary Ann Hopkins, dau. of Stephen Hopkins who is surety. p. 105.

9 December 1793. Peter WEST and Joanna White, who consents. Sur. Edward West. Wit. Elizabeth West, Tarpley White, Elizabeth White. p. 105.

10 January 1789. Whitlow WEST and Elizabeth Beall, who consents. Elizabeth is daughter of Millie Richardson. Sur. Drury West. Wit. George Winston. p. 105.

3 January 1697. James WESTBROOK and Elizabeth Puckett. Deeds, etc., 1697-1699. p. 96.

10 July 1793. Jacob WHEATON and Polly Davis, of lawful age. Sur. and Wit. Smith Blakey. p. 105.

14 February 1791. Richard WHEELIN and Rebecca Goodwin. Sur. C. Copland. p. 105.

15 June 1784. James WHITE and Nancy Bryant, who consents. Sur. William Harwood. p. 105.

10 August 1784. John WHITE and Licy Stone. Sur. Jacob Lockett. p. 105.

5 February 1806. Lewis WHITE and Nancy Scott. George Williamson certifies Nancy is the daughter of William Scott and is a free born woman. p. 105.

22 June 1789. Samuel WHITE and Mrs. Rhoda Spencer, who consents. Sur. Charles W. Soule who certifies Rhoda is over 21. Wit. ------ Whitfield. p. 105.

10 July 1795. Thomas WHITE and Sarah Welsh, of lawful age. Sur. Morton Welsh. Wit. John Lesslie. p. 105.

23 June 1803. Matthew WHITING and Susan Nelson, dau. of Robert Nelson who consents. Sur. Nathaniel Nelson who makes oath Susan is over 21. p. 105.

22 November 1806. John WHITIS and Sally Tuning. Sur. Reuben Hawes who makes oath Salley is over 21. p. 105.

6 June 1795. John WIDEWITT and Nancy Wilsford, who consents. Sur. Ellison Martin. Wit. Mary Martin and Robert Turner. p. 105.

17 February 1798. Hezekiah L. WIGHT and Nancy Leeds. Sur. Jedediah Leeds. p. 106.

7 February 1700. Joseph WILKINSON and Priscilla Skerme. Deeds, Wills, etc., 1697-1704. p. 243.

7 January 1706. Richard WILKINSON and Martha Cox. Deeds & Wills, 1706-1709. p. 67.

23 December 1791. Andrew WILLIAMS and Betsey Howel, who consents. Sur. and Wit. Joseph Harrel. p. 106.

28 February 1789. Edward WILLIAMS and Mary Woodcock, who consents. Sur. Joseph Laughay. Wit. John Burns, Andrew ------, Samuel Dyer. p. 106.

7 January 1783. Jesse WILLIAMS and Mary Harwood. Sur. Thomas Williams. p. 106.

31 August 1790. John WILLIAMS and Susanna Wray. William Wray consents for Susanna; no relationship stated. Sur. Macon Whitfield. Wit. Peter Sharp and Thomas Binford, Jr. p. 106.

16 December 1797. John WILLIAMS and Ann Clark, who consents. Sur. Claiborne West. Wit. Whitlow West. p. 106.

12 January 1801. John WILLIAMS and Edna Redford, dau. of Lucy Redford who consents. Sur. Josiah Bullington who makes oath Lucy is over 21. Wit. Edna Redford and John Barret. p. 106.

27 December 1808. John WILLIAMS and Elizabeth Lindsay. Sur. William Childrey who makes oath Elizabeth is over 21. p. 106.

14 September 1787. Philip WILLIAMS and Nancy Wade. Sur. Edward Wade. p. 106.

12 December 1791. Powell WILLIAMS and Nancy Smoot. Sur. Benjamin Smoot. p. 106.

12 October 1703. Robert WILLIAMS and Elizabeth Benskin. Deeds, Wills, etc., 1697-1704. p. 351.

31 July 1788. Rowland WILLIAMS and Elizabeth Dedman. Sur.
John Williams. p. 106.

5 October 1803. Samuel WILLIAMS and Jane Johnson, dau. of
Emanuel Johnson who is surety. p. 106.

9 October 1786. Thomas WILLIAMS and Jane Charlton, dau. of
Sarah Gilbert who consents. Sur. Jacob Ego. Wit. Susanna
Rukney. p. 106.

8 May 1790. William WILLIAMS and Sarah Miller, dau. of William
and Sarah Miller who consent. Sur. Aminadab Miller. Wit. John
Lacy and John Jordan. p. 106.

13 March 1794. William C. WILLIAMS and Alice Grymes Burwell,
who consents. Sur. Archibald Blair. Wit. F. Egglestone.
p. 106.

10 May 1796. Dabney WILLIAMSON and Lucy Burton. Sur. William
Burton. p. 106.

20 April 1782. Jacob WILLIAMSON and Mary Anderson. Sur. James
Anderson. p. 106.

26 March 1785. Thomas WILLIAMSON and Judith Parsons. Nathaniel
Clarke, guardian of Judith, consents for her. Sur. Edward
Miller. p. 107.

19 May 1807. Curthbert WILLIS and Sally Gentry. Note: This
bond probably lost since index was made in 1916. p. 107.

9 February 1786. William WILLIS and Mary Lankaster, dau. of
Joseph Lankaster who consents. Sur. Samuel Alley. Wit.
Cuthbery Willis (?) p. 107.

Before 20 August 1707. John WILSON, Jr. and widow of William
Chambers. Orphans Court, 1677-1739. p. 49.

9 December 1789. Charles WINEGARDNER and Elizabeth Henley.
Sur. Francis Gaddy. Wit. John Crawford, Mary Crawford, Turner
Morris. p. 107.

13 December 1797. Isaac WINFREY and Gracy Glenn, who consents.
Sur. Richardson Glenn. Wit. William Richardson and James
Talley. p. 107.

2 January 1784. John WINFREY and Elizabeth Owen. Sur. Thomas
Owen. p. 107.

9 September 1808. Charles Lewis WINGFIELD and Eliza Wilson.
Sur. Thomas Wilson. p. 107.

18 March 1807. John WINN and Polly Johnson, dau. of Benjamin
Johnson who is surety. p. 107.

March 1785. Peter WINN and Sarah King, who consents. Sur.
Charles Toler. p. 107.

17 December 1796. Thomas WINN and Anne Ellis, dau. of Susannah
Ellis who consents. Sur. Jesse Curd. Wit. Obediah Ellis.
p. 107.

13 March 1799. Edward WINSTON and Woody W. Harrison. David
Bradley, guardian of Woody, consents for her. Sur. and Wit.
John G. Winston. p. 107.

8 October 1794. Isaac WINSTON and Elizabeth Burton. Sur.
William Burton. p. 107.

15 March 1802. William WINSTON and Patsey Mosby. Sur. William
Mosby. p. 107.

26 November 1806. Charles WITHERS and Rhoda Wade. Sur. Ignatus
H. Allen who makes oath Rhoda is over 21. p. 107.

1688. William WITHERS and Elizabeth Bullington, widow of Robert
Bullington. Deeds, Wills, etc., 1688-1697. p. 20.

3 June 1795. William WOBBLETON and Susannah Sneed, dau. of
Charles Sneed who is surety. p. 107.

3 May 1787. Abraham WOMACK and Susanna Jolley, widow, who
consents. Sur. John Edwards. Wit. John Williamson and Richard
Throgmorton. p. 107.

23 November 1796. Abraham WOMACK and Mary Dailey. Sur. Daniel
Dumas. p. 108.

14 January 1791. Basil WOOD and Peggy Richardson. Sur. William
Richardson. Wit. George Davenport and John Mayleigh. p. 108.

7 December 1807. Elijah WOOD and Angela Barnett. (free people
of color). Sur. Adam Floyd. p. 108.

18 December 1789. Isaac WOOD and Abby Scott. Sur. Randolph
McGee. p. 108.

16 May 1794. Leighton WOOD and Mary Younghusband, dau. of Sarah
Younghusband who consents. Sur. John Tucker. Wit. John
Thompson and Zach. Rowland. p. 108.

Between 1688-1689. Moses WOOD and Elizabeth Farguson. Deeds,
Wills, etc., 1688-1697. p. 97.

3 June 1709. Moses WOOD and Mary Cox, dau. of Barth. Cox. Deeds
& Wills, 1706-1709. p. 188.

Before 5 October 1725. Richard WOOD and Anne Williamson, widow
of George Williamson. Orphans Court, 1677-1739. p. 54.

19 December 1792. Henry WOODCOCK and Salley Wade, dau. of Ann
Wade who consents. Sur. George Robinson. Wit. John Sweeny
and Thomas Wade. p. 108.

2 February 1808. Henry WOODCOCK and Ersley Jordan, dau. of
Noble Jordan who is surety. p. 108.

15 August 1796. Micajah WOODDY and Elizabeth Allen, wid. of
Littleberry Allen. Sur. William Spur. p. 108.

2 April 1798. James WOODFIN and Elizabeth Binford. Sur. Moses
Woodfin. Wit. Martha Warriner and Elizabeth Binford. p. 108.

23 September 1795. Moses WOODFIN and Martha Binford, widow,
who consents. Sur. James Warriner. p. 108.

31 August 1801. Moses WOODFIN and Susanna Garthright, who consents
and states she is over 21. Sur. James Warinner. Wit. Trueman
Warinner. p. 108.

28 August 1790. Thomas WOODFIN and Nancy Allen Sharpe, ward of
John James Woodfin who consents and is surety. p. 108.

19 May 1802. Thomas WOODFIN and Sophia Pleasants, dau. of
Elizabeth Pleasants who states Sophia is of lawful age. Sur.
and Wit. Gervas Storrs. p. 108.

25 November 1793. Daniel WOODSON and Nancy Gathright, who
consents. William Gathright certifies Nancy is his daughter
and is over 21. Sur. Obediah Gathright. Wit. John Miller
and William Clark. p. 108.

1691. Robert WOODSON and Sarah Lewis. Deeds, Wills, etc., 1688-
1697. p. 357.

20 July 1798. Thomas WOODSON and Elizabeth Redford, dau. of John
Redford who is surety. p. 108.

18 September 1795. William WOODSON and Milly Redford, dau. of
John Redford who consents and is surety. William is son of
Joseph Woodson of Goochland County who consents for him. Wit.
William Pledge, Richard Redford, Robert Woodson. p. 108.

8 February 1806. Charles WOODWARD and Catharine S. Ellis. Sur.
John S. Ellis who makes oath Catharine is over 21. p. 108.

28 January 1790. John WOODWARD and Jane Ellis, dau. of Joseph Ellis who consents. Sur. Henry Ellis. Wit. John Watson. p. 108.

18 September 1797. William WOODWARD and Sarah Bisset, who consents. Sur. Lyddall Clopton. p. 108.

3 January 1798. Elisha WOODY and Nancy Laughlin. Sur. James Bingham. p. 108.

7 September 1785. Samuel WOODY and Mrs. Elizabeth Denis. Sur. Henry Woody. p. 108.

7 January 1795. William WORSHAM and Sarah M. Gathright, who consents. Sur. Obediah Wade. Wit. O. Gathright and Joseph Wade. p. 109.

13 October 1792. James WRAY and Ann Deane, who consents. Sur. Francis Vanet. Wit. John Darrons. p. 109.

8 March 1790. Barnard WRIGHT and Judy Oakley, dau. of John Oakley who consents and is surety. p. 109.

7 June 1786. John WRIGHT and Anne Puryear, dau. of Margaret Puryear who consents. Sur. Reuben Puryear. Wit. John Bowles and Jesse Puryear. John Wright of Hanover County. p. 109.

30 October 1792. James YOAKELEY and Judy Yeats, who consents. Judy is daughter of Lucy Heath. Sur. John Williamson. Wit. Jeames Green and Barret Right. p. 111.

10 January 1807. James YOUNG and Susan Roberts. Sur. William Davidson who makes oath Susan is over 21. p. 111.

18 November 1806. Richard YOUNG and Margaret Anderson, dau. of James Anderson who consents. Sur. John Williamson. Wit. George Watt. p. 111.

27 November 1792. William YOUNG and Lucy Depriest, who consents. Sur. Knowles Giles. p. 111.

BLAKEY, Cont'd.
Nancy ... 85
Prudence Watkins ... 58

BLALOCK
Elizabeth ... 8
Nancy ... 29
Sarah ... 2

BLANCHEIL
Ann ... 19

BLANKENSHIP
Martha ... 80

BLITH
Hannah ... 5

BLOUNT, BLUNT
Mary ... 29
Susanna ... 5

BOCKINS
Susan ... 32

BOLES
Fanny ... 41

BOLTON
Catharine ... 35

BOOTH
Elizabeth ... 25

BOOZE
Eliza ... 64

BOTTOM
Elizabeth ... 24
Lenora ... 65
Molley ... 81
Susanna ... 33

BOTTOMLY
Jane ... 2

BOUGHS
Peggy ... 27

BOWERS
Betsey ... 1
Nancy ... 86

BOWES
Mary ... 57

BOWLES
Mary ... 44
Sally ... 16
Susanna ... 43

BOWMAN
Kitchora ... 48

BOYCE
Sarah ... 76

BOYD
Effany ... 2

BRACK
Martha ... 26

BRACKER
Fanny ... 22

BRACKET, BRACKETT
Betsey ... 8
Charity ... 5
Lucy ... 32
Sally ... 25

BRANCH
Obedience ... 20
Priscilla ... 77
Tabitha ... 17
Verlinche ... 10
Verlynche ... 36
Widow of ... 75

BRANSFORD
Agness ... 61

BRAZEAL
Patsey ... 23
Susanna ... 25

BREEDEN
Sally ... 25

BRENT
Elizabeth J. ... 15

BRIDGEWATER
Agness ... 37
Catharine ... 36
Dolly ... 19
Hester ... 10
Molley ... 42
Susanna ... 49
Susannah ... 19

BRIGHTWELL
Lucy ... 50

BRITAIN, BRITTAIN
Louisa ... 23
Nancy ... 47
Patsy ... 29
Salley ... 47
Sarah ... 26

BRITTON
Elizabeth ... 23
Lucy ... 74
Polley Lewis ... 22

BROMFIELD
Rosetta ... 88

BROMWELL
Mary ... 12

BROWN, BROWNE
Betty ... 15
Elizabeth ... 63,79
Judith ... 77
Judy ... 6
Patsey Cauley ... 85
Precilla ... 81
Temperence ... 6

BROWNING
Elizabeth ... 33
Mary ... 86
Mary Ann ... 30
Rebecca ... 22

BRUMFIELD
Patsey ... 12
Rosetta ... 33

BRYAN
Prescilla ... 28
Sarah ... 62

BRYANT
Nancy ... 91

BRUCKNER
Polley ... 43

BULLINGTON
Elizabeth ... 94
Lucy ... 36

BULLINGTON, Cont'd.
Martha ... 87
Mary ... 23
Sarah ... 74

BURNETT
Frances W. ... 81

BURNS
Lucy ... 67
Sally ... 70

BURROUGHS
Elinor ... 38

BURTON
Ann ... 81
Daughter of ... 41
Elizabeth ... 50,73,94
Frances ... 51
Lucy ... 68,93
Mary ... 63
Nancy F. ... 76
Rachel ... 87
Sarah ... 89
Susannah ... 81
Tabitha ... 78

BURWELL
Allice Grymes ... 93

BYONS
Frances ... 29

C

CAMMEL
Sarah ... 72

CAMPBELL
Elizabeth ... 6
Lucy ... 53

CANNON
Hester ... 17
Judith ... 14

CANY
Victoire Celeste ... 91

CAPEHEART
Barbara ... 9

CARLILE, CARLISLE
Elizabeth ... 57
Rachel ... 22

CARREL
Nancy ... 34

CARSEREAN
Nancy ... 78

CARTER
Elizabeth ... 10,33,41
Elizabeth G. ... 8
Elizabeth Wray ... 80
Frances ... 63
Judy ... 48
Lucy ... 83
Mary E. ... 46
Nancy ... 70,75
Polly ... 73
Polley P. ... 78
Rebecca ... 80
Salley ... 68
Susanna ... 14

CASSEY
Elizabeth ... 66

CASTEL
Sarah 22

CAUTHERN
Mary 11

CAWTHAN
Ruth 70

CAWTHON
Sally 8

CAWTHORNE
Rhoda 50

CEE
Elizabeth 41

CHAMBERS
Widow of 93

CHANDLER
Polley 1,45

CHAPMAN
Jane 68

CHAPPELL
Nancy 83

CHARLES
Mary 82
Widow of 63

CHARLTON
Jane 93

CHILDERS
Ann 1,55
Mary 84
Phebe 46

CHILDRESS
Fanny 37
Judith 80

CHOCKLEY
Frances 43

CLARK, CLARKE
Alice 27
Ann 22,62,92
Anne 55
Betsey 75
Charity 72
Elizabeth 20
Fanny 16
Frances 66
Jane 25
Judith 80
Martha 91
Mary 59
Mary Ann 11
Mildred 24
Patty 18
Sally 30,66,76
Sarah 27,63

CLAXTON
Martha 61

COBBS
Susannah H. 42

COCKE
Agness 13
Eliza F. 21
Elizabeth 16,70
Lucy 78
Martha 67
Nancy 65
Betsey 7
Rebecca 46

COCKE, Cont'd.
Salley 77
Sally Webb 25
Theodocia 90

COLE
Nancy 63

COLEMAN
Elizabeth W. 67

COLLINS
Ann 81
Jane 55
Judith 12

CONAND
Mary 4

COOK
Temperance 41

COOTES
Sarah 44

COPLAND
Mary 12

CORNET
Elizabeth 77
Rebecca 11
Susanna 36

COTTRELL
Judith 13

COURTNEY
Rachel 11

COUTTS
Mary L. 34

COWLEY
Elizabeth 48

COX
Judith 34
Martha 92
Mary 6,95

CRADDOCK
Lucy 62
Mary 38

CRAIN
Jenny 86

CRAWFORD
Jane 71

CRESSY
Katherine 66

CROUCH
Elizabeth 79

CROXTON
Susanna 59

CRUMP
Rosanna T. 49

CURD
Mary 54

CURLE
Salley 51

D

DABNEY
Charity 85

DAILEY, DAILY
Druscilla 65
Fanny 72
Kesiah 81
Mary 94

DANFORTH
Mary 29

DARRONS
Elizabeth O. 21

DAVENPORT
Frances 90
Keziah 4
Lucy 2
Nancy 90

DAVID
Lucy 75

DAVIS
Catherine 13
Jenny 81
Mary 20,21
Nancy 6,11
Polly 91

DAY
Elizabeth 16

DEAN, DEANE
Aggy 40
Ann 96
Elizabeth 54
Milley 9

DEDMAN
Elizabeth 93

DELAPLANCHE
Adelaide E. 34

DENIS, DENNIS
Elizabeth 96
Sarah 20

DEPRIEST
Betsey Jackson 23
Lucy 96
Martha 68

DERROM
Rasilla 43

DOBBS
Rebecca 68

DOLLARD
Anne 43

DOLLY 90

DONNELLY
Mary 24

DORISCH
Martha 73

DOUGLAS
Bethenia 90
Jane 27

DOVE
Julia Lee 43

DRAKE
Salley 66

DREWING		
Mary Ann	25	
DRUMMOND		
Peggy	82	
DUDLEY		
Frances	74	
DUMASS		
Elizabeth	35	
DUNELWEN		
Ann	64	
DUNN		
Margaret	90	
DUNNABERRY		
Regina	43	
DUPRAY		
Margaret	89	
DURHAM		
Janie	19	
Margaret	18	
DUVAL, DUVALL		
Elizabeth	38,43	
Lucy	69	
Nancy	81	
Philadelphia	28	
Polley	67	
Rebecca	75	
Sally	22	

E

EARNEST	
Pamela	23
EAST	
Ann	46
ECHO, ECHOE	
Elizabeth	9
Sarah	89
EDWARDS	
Martha	83
EGE	
Elizabeth	62
Sally	52
ELAM	
Frances	64
Mary	30,40
ELERSON	
Agness	87
ELLIOTT	
Ann	63
Betsey	56
ELLIS	
Anne	94
Catharine S.	95
Edith	42
Elizabeth	8,18,29,71,89
Hanna	59
Jane	24,96
Lucy	4
Mary	68
Nancy	29
Susanna	29,56
ELLISON, ELLYSON	
Catharine S.	86
Rita Ann	87

ELMORE	
Elizabeth	18
EMERY	
Patsey	40
EMMORY	
Lucy	78
ENRUFTY, ENROUGHTY	
Elizabeth	84
Martha	72
EUBANK	
Anne	13
Frances	22
Mary	35,43
Sarah	20
Sarah Mitchell	85
Sukey	15
EVANS	
Anna	68
Salley	48
Sally	11
EYRES	
Jane	34
Margaret	45

F

FARGUSON	
Elizabeth	94
FARIS, FARISS	
Crania	31
Elizabeth	41
FARNER	
Polly	86
FARRAR	
Anne	41
Sarah	73
FERGUSON	
Sarah	31
FERRIS	
Elizabeth	16
FIELD	
Mary	47
FINNY	
Sarah	87
FLEMING	
Elizabeth Carter	52
FLEMMON	
Rhoda	82
FLINT	
Magdaline	56
Margaret	66
FLOYD	
Ann	82
FORD, FORDE	
Dolley	33
Elizabeth	77
Lucy	87
Nancy	39
Polley	36
Sally	91
FORREST	
Mary	3

FOSTER	
Lucy	51
Nancy	47
Sally	17
FOUSHEE	
Isabella	72
FRANCES, FRANCIS	
Ann	24
Elizabeth	24
Frances	47
Kitty	33
Susanna	3
FRANKLIN	
Anna	54
Barbery	86
Coley	80
Elizabeth	1,44
Martha	42
Patsey	88
Phobe	13
Sally	12
Sarah	53
Susanna	86
FRAYSER	
Elizabeth	82
Elizabeth H.	18
Fanny	87
Lucy	14
Nancy	62
Patsey	43
FREEMAN	
Agness	44
Elizabeth	2
Franky	18
Nancy	38
Susanna	84
FRENCH	
Anne	67
Dolly	18
FULLGHAM	
Frances	60
FUSSELL	
Elizabeth	17
Jane	90
Mary	6
Polly Adams	88
Ursley	5

G

Gadberry	
Elizabeth	38
Sally	83
William	44
GALDEN	
Theodocia	27
GALT	
Eliza	82
Mary	24
GAMMON	
Sally	67
GANTZ	
Mary	39
GARDNER	
Anne	11
Elizabeth	67

GARTHRIGHT
  Agnes   10
  Elizabeth   8,35
  Fanny   49
  Mary   37
  Nancy   36,90
  Phobe   37
  Polly   35
  Susanna   95

GARY
  Elizabeth   85

GATEBY
  Jane   46

GATHRIGHT
  Agness   79
  Elizabeth   79
  Elizabeth M.   74
  Jane   22,35
  Jane M.   16
  Nancy   95
  Polly   35
  Sally   86
  Sarah M.   96

GAY
  Ann Thomas   37

GENNETT
  Betsey   30
  Maria   73
  Sally   32
  Susanna   80

GENTRY
  Mary   40
  Sally   93

GEOGHEGAN
  Mary Taylor   37

GEORGE
  Elizabeth W.   72

GIBBS
  Milley   71

GILCHRIST
  Janett   70

GILES
  Judith   69
  Lucy   20

GILL
  Molley   48

GLASS
  Sarah   55

GLENN
  Betsey Ann   25
  Gracy   93
  Jane   70
  Mary   30,50
  Sarah   10

GODFREY
  Mary   30

GOINE
  Anne   59

GOING
  Milley   40

GOOD, GOODE
  Elizabeth   58,70
  Jane   73
  Martha   19,72
  Mary   17,46

GOOD, Cont'd.
  Mildred   47
  Obedience   31

GOODWIN
  Rebecca   91

GOWER
  Tabitha   39

GOYNE
  Elizabeth   88
  Mary   17
  Nancy   17

GRANTLAND
  Catherine   15

GRAVES
  Elizabeth   56
  Nancy   2

GRAVITT
  Milly   5

GREEN
  Betsey   29
  Darcus   52
  Patsy   35
  Sarah   83

GREGORY
  Mary   18

GRIFFIN
  Nancy   59
  Susanna   36,80

GRINSTEAD
  Elizabeth   66
  Nancy   14

GRUBB
  Sarah   43

GUNN
  Arriana   55
  Harriet   87

H

HAIRE
  Nancy   42

HALES
  Betsy   20

HALL
  Nancy   39

HALLOCK
  Phobe   35

HAMBLETT
  Darkis   89
  Elizabeth   64

HANCOCK
  Joane   40
  Sarah   61

HARDEN
  Aggy   51
  Eleanor   6

HARDING
  Judah   81

HARDYMAN
  Sarah   62

HARE
  Catharine   81

HARLOE
  Elizabeth   81

HARLOW
  Patcey   30
  Sarah   45

HARRIS
  Michall   48

HARRISON
  Sally Carter   56
  Sarah   59
  Woody W.   94

HARVIE
  Gabriella   71

HARWOOD
  Bathsheba   54
  Elizabeth   9,16,37
  Frances   1
  Lucy   4
  Mary   92
  Nancy   17
  Patsey   79
  Polly Winston   43

HATCHER
  Martha   28

HAYES
  Annie D.   56

HAYNES
  Elizabeth   23
  Frances   22

HAZLEGROVE
  Naomey   15

HAZLEWOOD
  Mary   49,88
  Nancy   44
  Prudence   49

HEATH
  Elizabeth   87

HEISLER
  Mary   13

HENLEY
  Elizabeth   93
  Lucy   65
  Nancy   5,52
  Sarah   31

HENROTTA
  Nancy   11

HENRY
  Anna   72
  Betsy   4

HERBERT
  Sally   7

HETH
  Eliza   47
  Eliza Agness P.   20

HEWLETT
  Betsey   40
  Joanna   38

HIBDON
  Mary   30

HILL
Anne	69
Judith	13
Susanna	89

HOBSON
Betsey	16
Frances	16
Kesiah	33
Maria	13

HODGES
| Martha | 13 |
| Sarah | 69 |

HODGSON
| Charlotte Matilda | 45 |

HOGANS
| Rebecca | 65 |

HOGG
Makey	84
Rebecca	21
Sarah	4
Susannah	83

HOLAWAY
| Agness | 32 |

HOLBERT
| Polly | 14 |
| Sally Taylor | 19 |

HOLLAND
| Sarah | 74 |

HOLLIS
| Elizabeth | 60 |

HOLLOWAY
| Ann Carter | 8 |
| Susanna | 30 |

HOLMAN
Elizabeth	89
Jane	70
Keturah	91
Milley	45
Mourning	28

HOLMES
| Milly | 43 |
| Sus. | 78 |

HOLOWAY
| Lydia | 39 |

HOMES
| Patsey | 10 |
| Sarah | 6 |

HOOKER
| Ann | 20 |
| Lucy | 39 |

HOOPER
| Elizabeth | 68 |
| Susanna | 29 |

HOPKINS
| Eliza | 67 |
| Mary Ann | 91 |

HOSHER
| Peggy | 21 |

HOUAL
| Rebecca | 7 |

HOWEL
| Betsy | 92 |

HOWERTON
Elizabeth	79
Frances	47
Polly	75

HOY, HOYE
| Ann | 63 |
| Margaret | 55 |

HUBBARD
| Martha | 27 |
| Mary | 53 |

HUDDLESY
| Sarah | 18 |

HUDSON
Elizabeth	90
Elizabeth Ann	82
Luky	9
Sarah	53

HUES
| Widow of | 61 |

HUGHES
Alsey	31
Easter	24
Frances	7
Judith	13
Mary	13,19,38
Polley	6

HUGHSON
| Joane | 3 |

HUMPHRIES
| Mary | 24 |

HUNDLEY
| Rachael | 7 |
| Sarah | 84 |

HUTCHING
| Sary | 34 |

HUTCHINS
| Dorithea | 56 |

HUTCHINSON
| Elizabeth | 21 |

HUTSON
| Mary | 49 |

HYLLIARD
| Patsey | 58 |

HYLTON
| Mehetible | 25 |

I

INNES
| Catherine | 1 |

INNIS
| Sally | 84 |

IRVING
| Elizabeth | 52 |

J

JACKSON
| Rebekah | 46 |
| Sally | 42 |

JAMES
| Christian | 9 |
| Milley | 83 |

JAQUELIN
| Elizabeth | 11 |

JARMAN
| Jane | 21 |

JEFFERSON
| Mary | 8,58 |

JEFFS
| Susanna | 54 |

JENNINGS
| Mary | 33 |

JENNY | 66 |

JOHNSON
Frances	2
Jane	70,93
Jemima	9
Lucy	28
Martha	38
Mary	45
Polly	22,94
Sally	42
Sarah	33,59
Susanna	37

JOLLEY
| Susanna | 94 |

JONES
Betsey	80,81
Chloe	78
Elizabeth	32,86
Jemima	77
Lucretia	17
Margarett	49
Martha	41
Mary	50,62
Nancy L.M.	88
Patsy	80
Priscilla	77
Rebecca	2
Sally	51
Sarah	44
Susanna	87
Tempe	7

JORDAN
Elizabeth	40,77
Ersley	95
Martha	1
Nancy	5

JUDE
| Mary | -12 |
| Nancy | 58 |

JUILLS
| Mary | 7 |

K

KAY
| Margaret | 62 |

KEEP
| Nancy | 58 |

KEESEE
| Elizabeth | 83 |

KELLY, KELLEY
Elizabeth	59
Martha	73
Nancy	27
Phebe	76
Salley	53
Susanna	39

KENDRICK
Elizabeth ... 66

KENNON
Elizabeth ... 73
Martha ... 61
Mary ... 9,23
Nancy ... 68

KENT
Jemima ... 67

KERSEY
Kuzzy ... 87

KING
Catharine ... 87
Elizabeth ... 26
Sarah ... 94

KNOWLES
Bethenia ... 36

L

LACEY
Sarah ... 79

LANCASTER
Letitia ... 24
Lucy ... 63

LANKASTER
Mary ... 93
Sally ... 63

LANKFORD
Anne ... 48

LAUGHLIN
Nancy
Tabitha B. ... 78

LAWRENCE
Anne ... 4
Elizabeth ... 59

LAWSON
Frances ... 57

LEE
Harriot ... 55

LEEDS
Nancy ... 92

LEIPER
Lucy ... 60

LEISCESTER
Grisilda ... 80

LENLEY
Mary ... 47

LENNARD
Martha ... 78

LENOX
Lucy ... 16

LEONARD
Polly ... 19

LEPETTIT
Lucy ... 88

LESTER
Dorcas ... 88

LEWIS
Alice ... 50

LEWIS, Cont'd.
Eliza ... 26
Elizabeth ... 85
Jamima ... 76
Lucy ... 16
Martha ... 56
Polly ... 56
Sally ... 58
Sarah ... 95
Susanna ... 60
Susanna M. ... 88
Widow ... 85

LIGGAN
Winnefred ... 10

LIGON, LIGGON
Elizabeth ... 40,57
Mary ... 3
Phebe ... 31

LINCH
Elizabeth ... 61

LINDSAY
Elizabeth ... 92
Susanna ... 73

LINNARD
Sarah ... 78

LIPSCOMB
Betsey ... 26
Salley ... 28

LORD
Sally W. ... 58

LOVING
Susanna ... 85

LOWARY
Nancy ... 87

LOWNES
Debby ... 67

LUCAS
Lydia ... 55
Mary ... 5
Milly ... 8
Polly ... 58

LUDSON
Elizabeth ... 46

LYNCH
Barbary ... 33

LYNN
Mary ... 80

LYON
Frances ... 31
Susanna ... 10

Mc

McALISTER
Grace ... 11

McALLISTER
Susanna ... 48

McCAW
Elizabeth ... 48

McGEE
Sally ... 17

McGHEE
Elizabeth ... 54
Susanna ... 54

McMEECAN
Patsey ... 39

McMILLAN
Sarah ... 21

M

MAGEE
Nancy ... 1

MALLORY
Anne ... 52

MALONY
Pinelope ... 87

MARCHAND
Clathila Millet ... 75

MARSHALL
Elizabeth ... 21
Lucy ... 3

MARSTON
Sarah ... 20

MARTIN, MARTYN
Elizabeth ... 51
Mary ... 14
Rebecah ... 26

MASCALL
Elizabeth ... 46

MATHEWS, MATTHEWS
Anne ... 62
Fanny ... 54
Martha ... 56
Mary ... 17
Rachel ... 23
Sarah ... 34
Susanna ... 58,68
Susannah ... 64

MATTOX
Maryann ... 40

MAUZEY
Maria ... 18
Precilla ... 85

MAXWELL
Catherine ... 7

MAYO
Eliza B. ... 34
Polly T. ... 4

MEADOWS
Rachill ... 78

MELTON
Levinia ... 10

METTART
Elizabeth ... 2

MEUX
Elizabeth ... 4

MEWES
Ann ... 37

MILES
Kitty ... 23

MILLER
Abethsheba ... 46
Ann ... 19
Dolly ... 82
Elizabeth ... 64,78

MILLER, Cont'd.
　Frances　　　　　50
　Judith　　　　　84
　Margaret　　　　62
　Martha　　　　　82
　Mary　　　　　　67
　Rebecca P.　　　42
　Sarah　　　　6,15,93

MILLS
　Charlotte　　　　80

MILNER
　Martha　　　　　71

MINOR
　Elizabeth　　　　3
　Nancy　　　　　33

MINSON
　Elizabeth　　　　30
　Lovoisy　　　　30

MITCHELL
　Sally　　　　　21

MOGAWAY
　Sarah　　　　　55

MONEY
　Elizabeth　　　　23

MONTGOMERY
　Nancy　　　　　55

MOODY
　Catharine　　　　60

MOORE
　Ann　　　　　　36

MORRIS, MORRISS
　Alley　　　　　83
　Amey　　　　　27
　Elizabeth　　　　47
　Judy　　　　　60
　Mary　　　　　65
　Nancy　　　　　47
　Rhoda　　　　　52
　Sally　　　　　10

MORSING
　Nancy　　　　　90

MOSBY, MOSEBY
　Betsey　　　　　1
　Martha　　　　　40
　Nancy　　　　　64
　Patsey　　　　1,94

MOSELEY
　Anney　　　　　19

MOURNING
　Katy　　　　　71
　Sally　　　　　17

MUNCAS
　Betsey　　　　　28
　Mary　　　　　27
　Sarah　　　　　83

MURPHEY
　Precilla　　　　9

MUSE
　Bittey　　　　　79

MYERS
　Susanna　　　　31

N

NAGLEY
　Elizabeth　　　　65

NEIGLEY
　Catherine　　　　21

NAILER
　Martha　　　　　72

MAILOR
　Elizabeth　　　　54
　Rachel　　　　　7

NANCE
　Tabitha　　　　83

NASH
　Nancy　　　　　66

NEALE
　Nancy　　　　　51

NEGLEY
　Dorothy　　　　12

NELSON
　Susan　　　　　92
　Susanna　　　　48

NEW
　Jane　　　　　23
　Mary　　　　　65

NEWCOMB
　Mary　　　　　58

NEWMAN
　Catharine　　　　75
　Elizabeth　　　　2
　Salley　　　　　30

NICHOLS
　Sarah　　　　　75

NICHOLSON
　Mary Ann　　　47

NICOLSON
　Arener　　　　14

NORMENT
　Milly　　　　　17

O

OAKLEY
　Judy　　　　　96
　Polly　　　　　15

OLIVER
　Catharine　　　　51

OMBERSON
　Mary　　　　　19

OMOHUNDRO
　Julilie　　　　27

ORECHER
　Harriot　　　　6

ORR
　Anna　　　　　80

OSBORNE
　Martha　　　　29

OSLIN
　Elizabeth　　　　14

OTEY
　Polley　　　　　50

OWEN
　Elizabeth　　　　93
　Jemimah　　　　54
　Martha　　　　　61
　Sally　　　　　14

P

PAGE
　Eliza Harriet　　56

PAINTER
　Sally　　　　　25

PANKEY
　Betsey Kinsey　　90

PARKE
　Catharine　　　　58

PARKER
　Anne　　　　　59
　Elizabeth　　　　79
　Martha　　　　　8
　Mary　　　　　14
　Mary H.　　　　70
　Sally　　　　　40
　Susannah　　　　48

PARRISH
　Nancy　　　　　33

PARSONS
　Judith　　　　93

PASLEY
　Huldak　　　　57
　Mary　　　　　76

PATE
　Elizabeth　　　　22

PATMAN
　Anne　　　　　83

PATRICK
　Hannah　　　　26

PATT　　　　　　46

PATTEN
　Salley　　　　　40

PATTESON
　Luvinia　　　　3

PAYNE
　Katy　　　　　50
　Sarah　　　　　73

PEARCE
　Ann　　　　　18
　Elizabeth　　　　5

PEARMAN
　Jane　　　　　26

PEARSON
　Beckie Walton　　89
　Betsey　　　　　13
　Nancy　　　　　81

PECK
　Anne　　　　　68
　Salley　　　　　58

PEERMAN
　Mary　　　　　66

WILLIAMS, Cont'd
   Mary   14,49,65
   Nancy   45,59
   Sarah   72

WILLIAMSON
   Anne   95
   Eliza D.   66
   Jane   34
   Lucy   11
   Mary   13,52,70,79
   Prudence   69
   Rebecca   10,61
   Sally   20
   Sophia   79

WILLIS
   Betsey   71
   Frances   84
   Sarah   34

WILLS
   Ann   38

WILSFORD
   Nancy   92

WILSON
   Eliza   93
   Frances   12

WINSTON
   Anne   61
   Elizabeth   61
   Lucy   73
   Mary Ann   48
   Patsy   77
   Rebecca   3,41
   Sally   85

WISE
   Mary   86

WISEHAM
   Jane   64

WOMACK
   Elizabeth   41
   Martha   61
   Susanna   63

WOOD
   Catherine   53
   Lucretia   6
   Mary   53
   Sary   64

WOODCOCK
   Elizabeth   45,86
   Mary   92

WOODFIN
   Mary   37
   Sarah   35

WOODWARD
   Elizabeth   32
   Mary   64
   Rebecca   50

WOODY
   Franky   82

WOOLBANKS
   Frances   44
   Nancy   39

WORRELL
   Elizabeth   55

WORSHAM
   Elizabeth   54
   Frances   73
   Mary   42,54

WRAY
   Matilda   15
   Sally   66
   Susanna   92

WRIGHT
   Nancy   56
   Sarah   19

WYSE
   Charity   38

Y

YEATS
   Judy   96

YOUNGHUSBAND
   Mary   94